DIABETIC
AIR FRYER COOKBOOK
2022

For a Healthy and Energetic Life. **201+** Easy and Healthy Recipes for Your Air Fryer

30-Day Meal Plan | Take care of your Well-Being

EVELINE WHITE

TABLE OF CONTENTS

INTRODUCTION

Diabetes has become widespread in our society. This disease affects millions of people and can be fatal if not managed properly. Fortunately, there are things you can do to control blood sugar levels. One of the best ways is the use of an air fryer.

This guide will explain how air fryers are used for a diabetic diet and how it could help you. You will also learn how to make diabetic recipes using an air fryer. There are numerous benefits to the diabetic diet, but we need to learn about diabetic cooking.

The air fryer offers health benefits for those with diabetes. People with diabetes have to watch their diet and monitor their blood sugar levels. The Diabetic Air Fryer Cookbook gives a step-by-step guide to preparing healthy meals and snacks in the air fryer. This explains the benefits of a diabetic diet, how to use air fryers properly, and what people with diabetes are supposed to eat.

When you have diabetes, you must change your eating habits to help keep your blood sugar levels under control. You will lower your chances of getting heart disease and stroke by eating healthy foods and controlling high blood sugar levels with medication. Several types of food may not be safe for you, depending on which type of diabetes you have.

Many different types of diabetes can make your blood sugar spike, but often the diet that causes it is not known. This will teach you how to use an air fryer to control your diabetes with a low-carb diet.

Many myths surround the air fryer, but they all prove to be wrong once you take a deeper look at them. People believe that because the foods cooked in an air fryer are unhealthy, they should never be used by diabetes. This is a myth as the air fryer can cook quite well without compromising on taste and flavor.

An air fryer is a powerful kitchen equipment that allows you to cook food in a healthier way than regular cooking methods. You can use your air fryer for cooking foods traditionally fried or baked at lower temperatures and without any unhealthy fat or oil. This allows you to enjoy more variety in your diet and experience amazing tasting results.

You will find many different recipes that fit into your diabetic diet. You will learn how to include air-fried foods in your diet while maintaining a low carb diet. Most of the recipes include high protein and low carbohydrate foods, which keep your blood sugar in check.

Most of the recipes are simple to make to add them into your daily life easily. You can make all your favorite meals including, fried chicken legs, mashed potatoes, and macaroni and cheese.

Because some foods cause glucose to rise too quickly in the bloodstream, and some foods that cause glucose to fall too quickly, we understand that the perfect diet for diabetes is not an easy task. However, with a little research and our Diabetic Air Fryer Cookbook, you can make delicious meals without worrying about your meal controlling blood sugar levels.

Not only can you eat like a person with diabetes, but with our recipes, you can also make healthier dishes. This is the perfect solution because they allow you to cook without worrying about what you are going to eat when you are done.

This is designed to serve both as an introduction to the air fryer and as a guide to controlling diabetes through diet. You will get to know how easy it is to eat healthier meals by using your air fryer. Your health will thank you for it!

DIABETES & OBESITY

While many individuals may live with diabetes, there is a great deal unknown to those who have it and even more unknown to those who do not. Diabetes is an illness that can affect any individual, from children to the elderly, which is why all individuals need to understand what this condition is, how it can be prevented, and what to do if you are at a higher risk of developing it.

This will help you understand what diabetes is, why glucose and insulin levels become too high or too low, the first signs of type 2 diabetes, and how the long-term effects of this condition can put you at risk.

How Glucose & Insulin Work Together

Glucose is how body gets its energy from sugars in the foods you eat. Energy can also be obtained from the foods you eat broken down into sugar once in the body. Foods that provide high glucose levels to the body are carbohydrates such as bread and starchy vegetables like white potatoes and fruits. When the glucose or sugar is released from foods in the stomach, it then flows through to the intestines and is absorbed into the bloodstream. The glucose in the bloodstream and body is referred to as blood sugar or blood glucose. Insulin is the hormone responsible for pushing the glucose through the body to other cells to provide them with energy. If there is no present need for energy, then insulin stores excess glucose to be used later. Most of the cells that absorb the glucose are found in the muscles in the body.

Insulin is created through the beta cells located in the pancreas. Consuming sugar triggers the beta cells to release insulin, which notifies the other cells in the body to absorb the sugar for energy. If there is sugar left over once all the cells have been properly filled, the excess is kept in the liver and muscles as glycogen. The body can store enough glucose to energize you for an entire day.

When you go for a few hours without eating, the pancreas puts a hold on sending out insulin. Instead, alpha cells will start creating a glucagon hormone. This sends a signal to the liver that it needs to start breaking down stored glucose to energy.

The liver is also able to produce its glucose to send out and replenish cells with energy. It uses waste products, fats, and amino acids to create its glucose.

Diabetes take place when the body cannot produce enough insulin or produces too much insulin, which blood glucose levels are too high or significantly lower than what the average level should be. There is a large strain put on the pancreas when this occurs, which can cause serious damage to the pancreas. Type 2 diabetes often affects adults and is the most common type of diabetes while Type 1 diabetes is common among children.

1.2 Types of Diabetes

Type 1 Diabetes

Type 1 diabetes results from the body being unable to produce enough insulin to move glucose through the body. The immune system sends out a signal for other cells to attack the pancreas cells and is considered an autoimmune disease. This improper functioning of the immune system results in the body mistakenly attacking its cells, specifically the beta cells in the pancreas. When the cells responsible for creating insulin come under attack, they can no longer produce insulin. This causes glucose levels to remain elevated and, if they are not lowered, can cause damage vessels in the body responsible for carrying oxygen to the organs. This puts you at a higher risk of heart disease, stroke, heart attack, liver damage and kidney disease.

Type 2 Diabetes

It is the result of the body not responding to insulin as it is expected to. This condition can cause more insulin to be made when there is no need for it, or a lack of insulin being produced when it is needed. When this occurs, the pancreas can become severely damaged and cannot make the insulin the body needs. One of the first indications that you could develop type 2 diabetes is a diagnosis of prediabetes. This inability to properly respond to insulin production is called insulin resistance.

Gestational Diabetes

Developing gestational diabetes which is diabetes that occurred due to pregnancy (and often disappears after pregnancy) is a risk factor for developing diabetes at some point.

1.3 The Causes of Diabetes

Several factors can affect the body's glycemic response. Glycemic response refers to the length of time needed for the body to be affected by glucose once consumed. It is not uncommon for individuals to see a slight increase in glucose levels after one eats, but in a healthy person, these levels will shortly return to the normal fasting rate. Fasting glucose rates are those that occur in between meals. These rates can show whether the body has been able to lower glucose levels after a meal.

When fasting glucose levels remain high, the insulin is not working as it should in the body. Those with type 2 diabetes will see a significant increase in glucose levels that can remain high for an extended period. You have to understood that the glycemic response can be affected by several factors and not just by carbohydrates or sugars as once was believed. Instead it is now understood that all of the following factors impact the glycemic response:

- The type of carbohydrate

- Amount of that carbohydrate

- The type of sugar, either lactose, fructose, glucose, or sucrose.

- The starch (Is it resistant starch, amylose, or amylopectin?)

- How the food was prepared (cooking can break down some of its compounds)

- The type of food

- Food components (additional substances in food can affect digestion)

With so many factors affecting glucose levels in the body, it is easy to understand why type 2 diabetes a complex disorder is to manage.

When a person shows symptoms that they could develop type 2 diabetes are determined with prediabetes. This is when the blood sugar levels are elevated to a higher level than normal but not quite high enough to be considered diabetes. Those with prediabetes are at a greater risk of eventually developing type 2 diabetes within a five-year time frame. Those with prediabetes already show signs of insulin resistance and impaired tolerance and fasting of glucose.

Prediabetes does not present itself in individuals with noticeable signs or symptoms, however. The only way it is usually detected is when a doctor checks an individual's blood glucose levels or after a complication, like a heart attack, has occurred. This makes this condition so complex; it is virtually impossible to detect unless complications are already occurring. This is why it is important to know what can put you are great risk of developing prediabetes and type 2 diabetes.

Conditions that high risk of developing prediabetes according to the National Institute of Diabetes and Digestive and Kidney Disease can include:

- Obesity

- Abdominal Obesity

- High Blood Pressure

- High Levels of Triglycerides (fat)

- Low Levels of HDL Cholesterol (high-density lipoprotein or bad cholesterol)

Those at greatest risk are individuals who do not exercise regularly, have a history of type 2 diabetes in their family, have high levels of stress, smoke, or drink excessively.

1.4 Early Signs of Diabetes

While there are no early warning signs that indicate type 2 diabetes, certain side effects can be observed when glucose levels are too high. Though you may experience these symptoms if you don't have a current diagnosis with diabetes, these may not cause much alarm. Some of the symptoms of elevated glucose levels include:

- Excess glucose forces liquid to be extracted from the tissues in the body, which causes an individual to have to consume more liquids and increase the need to urinate.

- When liquid is being pulled from the tissues in the body, one area that can become seriously affected is the eyes. When there are high glucose levels in the body, individuals can experience temporary vision disturbances such as blurred vision.

- Since the cells in the body are unable to absorb glucose, this results in a loss of energy. This causes an individual to feel more hunger than the muscles and organs crave energy they are not receiving.

- Additionally, when the body is not receiving the energy it needs from glucose, individuals will become extremely fatigued.

- Individuals may notice darker areas on the skin, a condition called acanthosis nigricans. This condition can affect the neck, elbows, knuckles, and knees.

- Type 2 diabetes can result in low levels of insulin. This causes the body to burn its stored fat for energy and as a result can lead to weight loss.

- Those with type 2 diabetes will also notice it takes longer for wounds to heal or recover from infections. This inability to recover quickly from infections results from poor circulation in the body and nutrient deficiencies.

Individuals are encouraged to speak to their doctor if any of those conditions persist as diabetes can lead to additional complications. Hypoglycemia is a common condition that can cause:

- Feeling confused

- Dizziness

- Feeling faint

- Increase in heartbeat

- Sudden changes in mood

- Heart palpitations

- Unconsciousness

- Excessive sweating

- Being more clumsy

These symptoms are a result of glucose levels falling below 70 mg/dl. Milder hypoglycemia symptoms can often be suppressed quickly by drinking a cup of fruit juice or having some hard candies. If symptoms are left unattended, an individual can quickly suffer from coma or seizures.

Another serious condition that can occur as a result of type 2 diabetes is hyperglycemia. When the glucose levels in the body increase significantly without treatment, this can result in what is known as diabetic ketoacidosis. This condition occurs when ketones begin to get trapped in the blood, resulting in too acidic blood. An individual suffering from ketoacidosis may have difficulty breathing, dry mouth, nausea, vomiting and, in severe cases, coma. This condition can be fatal.

HEALTHY LIVING & AIR-FRYING

An air fryer is a cooking gadget that uses a reduced quantity of oil and dry air heated to a high temperature to cook food. Using an air fryer is quick as you don't need to cook your food for a long time; it heats the air quickly while the food cooks. You don't need to pre-heat or make any preparation before using an air fryer.

If you enjoy fried food but don't want to suffer the effect of eating trans-fat and artificial oils, then you should try cooking with an air fryer.

2.1 How an Air Fryer Works?

- Air fryers make a loud sound

- They are hands-on. You need to remove the basket and shuffle the food around after a few minutes

- The grate should always be in the basket to allow hot air to circulate

- You don't need to shut off the machine to pull out the basket for a peek; it shuts off automatically when the basket is out

- Always put the drawer all the way in

- The less food in the basket, the faster it cooks

- Some air fryer recipes call for a lower temperature; always check the recipe to determine what temperature is ideal.

2.2 Cooking in An Air Fryer?

Air fryers cook mostly dry foods, so it will be best to choose food that cooks well with dry heat (frying, baking, and roasting). Some examples of those foods are:

- Potatoes

- Fish, patted dry

- Chicken breast

- Crab

- Broccoli

- Brussels sprouts

- Carrots and peppers

- Cauliflower florets

2.3 Cooking in An Air Fryer for Beginners

Don't use cooking spray to grease the drawer

An air fryer's basket has a non-stick coating that will be damaged over time when sprayed with a cooking spray. Every air fryer states this clearly in the manual, so this is a reminder. Instead of cooking spray, rub your food with oil or rub your food with an oil saturated paper towel. Air frying a pre-fried frozen food doesn't require extra grease.

Don't add too much oil

Using excess oil isn't needed. You will end up seeing it in the drawer under the air fryer's grate. This might smoke if there is too much oil build-up. Some foods like frozen fried food don't even require more oil, while vegetables need just a little oil coating.

Don't forget to shake the basket

By shaking the basket occasionally, you ensure that the food is evenly cooked with the right amount of browning. Cooking large items requires that you flip the food rather than shake it.

Avoid oil with a low smoke point

Olive oil should be avoided because of its low smoke point. It will smoke at a high temperature and give the food a weird taster. Use grape seed oil or vegetable oil, and other high smoke point oils.

Don't overwhelm the drawer

Despite looking big, air fryers don't have a big capacity. To get the best results, make sure you don't overwhelm the fryer with too much food. Cook in batches instead.

Don't dump the hot content of the drawer into a plate/bowl

When getting your food out, make use of tongs. The removable grate in the basket contains excess oil; yanking out the basket tip to a platter will lead to greasy food, making a mess, and might even burn you.

Don't place hot drawer on the countertop

The bottom of your drawer will be hot when pulled out, so grab it by its handle and set it on a potholder or trivet to avoid damaging your countertop with heat. I've been a victim of this experience; avoid it.

Don't touch your air fryer while it's on

Never touch the exterior part of your air fryer until it is cool. The air fryer's back is very likely to get hot, so don't touch it with your bare hands.

Don't trust the timer totally

Some basket-style air fryers come with a dial you can use to set time. When the time is up, it makes a ping sound, and the machine automatically stops. Some air fryers may be off by a few minutes compared to a real-time clock or a phone's timer. Although it is usually not a big deal, you need to keep re-setting your timer until the food is done to your satisfaction. However, have it at the back of your mind that not all timers run correctly.

Don't multitask with something that requires your attention while running an air fryer

Air fryers are loud, and you can't just ignore the noise they make. If you are running an air fryer and you want to listen to your favorite songs or a podcast, don't even bother; you won't be able to concentrate. Maybe you can do that before or after cooking.

Cleaning Your Air Fryer

After every use, make sure you clean your air fryer to avoid making the unit smoke. If you don't enjoy cleaning, you are in luck because air fryers are easy to clean. You have to use a paper towel to wipe off the grate and drawer when it doesn't require thorough cleaning. You easily hand wash it if it is gunky. Check your product's manual to see if some parts of your air fryer are dishwasher safe.

2.4 Benefits of Using an Air Fryer

It is quick and energy-efficient

Oil use is 70% less than in a deep fryer

It has an automatic shut off

Cleaning is easy, and it is dishwasher safe

It is multipurpose (it can grill, roast, fry, and bake)

It is helpful for people following a diet

It makes tasty food

2.5 Healthy living & Healthy Eating Habits

Fat is an essential diet that plays a vital role in a healthy diet. Fats provide essential fatty acids and energy that are both important for the body. They help regulate cholesterol metabolism and maintain healthy skin. Dietary fats facilitate the absorption of fat-soluble vitamins and hormones and satisfying people's appetite.

Although fats and oil have their many functions, there is still evidence showing that a diet high in fat can lead to serious health problems such as heart disease, cancer, obesity, and diabetes complications. A high intake of cholesterol, trans fat, and saturated fat can increase one's risk of harmful fat levels.

A healthy intake of fat should be between 20% and 35% of total calories. It is advisable not to consume more than 35% of total calories to maintain a healthy diet.

We all know our body needs fat. You need to make sure you are not eating more than the required amount of fat as a person with diabetes. Also, it would help if you didn't eat fats that will harm your health. The right amount of fat will promote heart health, lower blood pressure, prevent blood clots, and aid in maintaining blood sugar levels.

Keeping a tab on the fat you eat can be tricky, but an air fryer can make it easier, as it reduces the amount of fats in your food.

DIABETICS AIR FRYER APPETIZERS AND SIDES

1. Buffalo Cauliflower

Preparation Time: 5 minutes
Cooking Time: 15 minutes
Servings: 4
INGREDIENTS:

- 1/2 cup Homemade buffalo sauce
- 1 head of cauliflower, cut bite-size pieces
- 1 tbsp. Butter melted
- 1 tsp. Olive oil
- Kosher salt & pepper, to taste

DIRECTIONS:

1. Put cooking oil on the air fryer basket.
2. In a bowl, add buffalo sauce, melted butter, pepper, and salt. Mix well.
3. Put the cauliflower bits in the air fryer and spray the olive oil over it. Let it cook at 400 F for 7 minutes.
4. Remove the cauliflower from the air fryer and add it to the sauce. Coat the cauliflower well.
5. Put the sauce coated cauliflower back into the air fryer.
6. Cook at 400 F, for 7-8 minutes or until crispy.
7. Take out from the air fryer and serve with dipping sauce.

NUTRITION: Calories 101 Carbohydrates 4g Protein 3g Fat: 7g

2. Mini Pizza

Preparation Time: 2 minutes
Cooking Time: 5 minutes
Servings: 1
INGREDIENTS:

- 1/4 cup Sliced olives
- 1 pita bread
- 1 tomato
- 1/2 cup Shredded cheese

DIRECTIONS:

1. Let the air fryer preheat to 350 F
2. Lay pita flat on a plate. Add cheese, slices of tomatoes, and olives.
3. Cook for five minutes at 350 F

4. Take the pizza out of the air fryer.
5. Slice it and enjoy

NUTRITION: Calories: 344 Carbohydrates: 37g Protein: 18g Fat: 13g

3. Egg Rolls

Preparation Time: 10 minutes
Cooking Time: 20 minutes
Servings: 3
INGREDIENTS:

- Coleslaw mix: half bag
- Half onion
- Salt: 1/2 teaspoon
- Half cups of mushrooms
- Lean ground pork: 2 cups
- One stalk of celery
- Wrappers (egg roll)

DIRECTIONS:

1. Put a skillet over medium flame, add onion and lean ground pork and cook for 5-7 minutes.
2. Add coleslaw mixture, salt, mushrooms, and celery to skillet and cook for almost five minutes.
3. Lay egg roll wrapper flat and add filling (1/3 cup), roll it up, seal with water.
4. Spray with oil the rolls.
5. Arrange in the air fryer for 6-8 minutes at 400F, flipping once halfway through.
6. Serve hot.

NUTRITION: Cal 245 Fat: 10g Carbs: 9g Protein: 11g

4. Chicken Nuggets

Preparation Time: 15 minutes
Cooking Time: 15 minutes
Servings: 4
INGREDIENTS:

- Olive oil spray
- 2 chicken breasts, cut into bite pieces (Skinless boneless)
- 1/2 tsp. of kosher salt& freshly ground black pepper to taste

- 2 tbsp. Grated parmesan cheese
- 6 tablespoons (whole wheat) Italian seasoned breadcrumbs
- 2 tablespoons Whole wheat breadcrumbs
- 2 teaspoons olive oil

DIRECTIONS:

1. Let the air fryer preheat for 8 minutes to 400 F
2. In a big mixing bowl, add panko, parmesan cheese, and breadcrumbs and mix well.
3. Sprinkle kosher salt and pepper on chicken and olive oil. Mix well.
4. Take a few pieces of chicken, dunk them into breadcrumbs mixture.
5. Put these pieces in an air fryer and spray with olive oil.
6. Cook for 8 minutes, turning halfway through.
7. Enjoy with kale chips.

NUTRITION: Calories: 188 Carbohydrates: 8g Protein: 25g Fat: 4.5g

5. Kale & Celery Crackers

Preparation Time: 10 minutes
Cooking Time: 20 minutes
Servings: 6
INGREDIENTS:

- One cups flax seed, ground
- 1 cup flax seed, soaked overnight, and drained
- 2 bunches kale, chopped
- 1 bunch basil, chopped
- 1/2 bunch celery, chopped
- 2 garlic cloves, minced
- 1/3 cup olive oil

DIRECTIONS:

1. Mix the ground flaxseed with the celery, kale, basil, and garlic in your food processor and mix well.
2. Add the oil and soaked flaxseed, then mix again, scatter in the pan of your air fryer, break into medium crackers and cook for 20 minutes at 380 degrees F.
3. Serve as an appetizer and break into cups.
4. Enjoy.

NUTRITION: Calories 143 Fat 1g Carbs 8g Protein 4g

6. Spanakopita Bites

Preparation Time: 10 minutes
Cooking Time: 15 minutes
Servings: 4
INGREDIENTS:

- 4 sheets phyllo dough
- 2 cups Baby spinach leaves
- 2 tablespoons Grated Parmesan cheese
- 1/4 cup Low-fat cottage cheese
- 1 teaspoon Dried oregano
- 6 tbsp. crumbled Feta cheese
- 2 tablespoons Water
- 1egg white only
- 1 teaspoon Lemon zest
- 1/8 teaspoon Cayenne pepper
- 1 tablespoon Olive oil
- 1/4 Kosher salt
- 1/4 freshly ground black pepper

DIRECTIONS:

1. Prepare a pot over high heat, add water and spinach, cook until wilted.
2. Drain it and cool for ten minutes. Squeeze out excess moisture.
3. In a bowl, mix cottage cheese, Parmesan cheese, oregano, salt, cayenne pepper, egg white, freshly ground black pepper, feta cheese, spinach, and zest. Mix it well or in the food processor.
4. Arrange one phyllo sheet on a flat surface. Spray with oil. Add the second sheet of phyllo on top—spray oil. Add a total of 4 oiled sheets.
5. Form 16 strips from these four oiled sheets. Add one tbsp of filling in one strip. Roll it around the filling.
6. Spray the air fryer basket with oil. Put eight bites in the basket, spray with oil. Cook for 12 minutes at 375°F until crispy and golden brown. Flip halfway through.
7. Serve hot.

NUTRITION: Calories 82 Fat 4g Protein 4g Carbohydrate 7g

7. Onion Rings

Preparation Time: 10 minutes
Cooking Time: 10 minutes

Servings: 4

INGREDIENTS:

- 1 egg whisked
- 1 large onion
- 1 1/2 cup Whole-wheat breadcrumbs: 1 and 1/2 cup
- 1 teaspoon Smoked paprika
- 1 cup Flour
- 1 teaspoon Garlic powder
- 1 cup Buttermilk
- Kosher salt and pepper to taste

DIRECTIONS:

1. Cut the stems of the onion. Then cut into half-inch-thick rounds.
2. In a bowl, add flour, pepper, garlic powder, smoked paprika, and salt. Then add egg and buttermilk. Mix to combine.
3. In another bowl, add the breadcrumbs.
4. Coat the onions in buttermilk mix, then in breadcrumbs mix.
5. Freeze these breaded onions for 15 minutes. Spray the fryer basket with oil spray.
6. Put onions in the air fryer basket in one single layer. Spray the onion with cooking oil.
7. Cook at 370 degrees for 10-12 minutes. Flip only, if necessary.
8. Serve with sauce.

NUTRITION: Calories: 205 Fat 5.5g Carbohydrates 7.5g Protein 18g

8. Delicata Squash

Preparation Time: 5 minutes
Cooking Time: 10 minutes
Servings: 2

INGREDIENTS:

- 1/2 tablespoon Olive oil
- 1 Delicata squash
- 1/2 teaspoon Salt
- 1/2 teaspoon Rosemary

DIRECTIONS:

1. Chop the squash in slices of 1/4 thickness. Discard the seeds.
2. In a bowl, add olive oil, salt, rosemary with squash slices. Mix well.
3. Cook the squash for ten minutes at 400 F. flip the squash halfway through.

4. Make sure it is cooked completely.
5. Serve hot.

NUTRITION: Calories: 69 Fat: 4g Carbs: 9g Protein 1g

9. Zucchini Parmesan Chips

Preparation Time: 10 minutes
Cooking Time: 20 minutes
Servings: 6

INGREDIENTS:

- 1/2 cup Seasoned, whole wheat Breadcrumbs
- 2 Thinly slices of zucchinis
- 1/2 cup (grated) Parmesan Cheese
- 1 egg whisked
- Kosher salt and pepper, to taste

DIRECTIONS:

1. Pat dry the zucchini slices so that no moisture remains.
2. In a bowl, whisk the egg with a few tsp. of water and salt, pepper. In another bowl, mix the grated cheese, smoked paprika (optional), and breadcrumbs.
3. Coat zucchini slices in egg mix then in breadcrumbs. Put all in a rack and spray with olive oil.
4. In a single layer, add in the air fryer, and cook for 8 minutes at 350 F.
5. Add kosher salt and pepper on top if needed, enjoy as a mid-day snack.

NUTRITION: Calories 101 Fat: 8g Carbs: 6g Protein: 10g

10. Roasted Corn

Preparation Time: 10 minutes
Cooking Time: 10 minutes
Servings: 4

INGREDIENTS:

- 4 corn ears
- 2 to 3 teaspoons Olive oil
- Kosher salt and pepper to taste

DIRECTIONS:

1. Clean the corn, wash, and pat dry.
2. Fit in the basket of air fryer, cut if need to.
3. Top with olive oil, kosher salt, and pepper.
4. Cook for ten minutes at 400 F.
5. Enjoy crispy roasted corn.

NUTRITION: Calories 28 Fat 2g Carbs 0 g Protein 7 g

11. Spinach Frittata

Preparation Time: 5 minutes
Cooking Time: 10 minutes
Servings: 4
INGREDIENTS:
- 1/3 cup of packed spinach
- 1 small chopped red onion
- 3 eggs
- Salt, pepper
- Shredded mozzarella cheese

DIRECTIONS:
1. Let the air fryer preheat to 180 C.
2. Get a skillet and place over a medium flame. Add oil, onion, cook until translucent, add spinach and sauté until half cooked.
3. Beat eggs and season with kosher salt and pepper—mix spinach mixture in it.
4. Cook in the air fryer for 8 minutes or until cooked.
5. Slice and Serve hot.

NUTRITION: Calories 124 Fat: 10.9g Carbs: 14.1g Protein: 16.9 g

12. Sweet Potato Fries

Preparation Time: 5 minutes
Cooking Time: 8 minutes
Servings: 2
INGREDIENTS:
- 1 sweet potato
- Pinch of kosher salt
- Fresh ground black pepper, to taste
- 1 tsp olive oil

DIRECTIONS:
1. Cut the peeled sweet potato in French fries. Coat with salt, pepper, and oil.
2. Cook in the air fryer for 8 minutes at 400 degrees F.
3. Cook potatoes in batches, in single layers.
4. Shake once or twice.
5. Serve with your favorite sauce.

NUTRITION: Calories: 60 Carbohydrates: 13g Protein: 1g Fat 6g

13. Kale Chips

Preparation Time: 3 minutes
Cooking Time: 5 minutes
Servings: 2
INGREDIENTS:
- 1 bunch of kale
- 1/2 tsp. of garlic powder
- 1 tsp. of olive oil
- 1/2 tsp. of salt

DIRECTIONS:
1. Let the air fryer preheat to 370 degrees F.
2. Cut the kale into small pieces without the stem.
3. In a bowl, add all ingredients with kale pieces.
4. Add kale to the air fryer.
5. Cook for three minutes. Toss it and cook for two minutes more.
6. Serve with any dipping.

NUTRITION: Calories: 37 Carbohydrates: 6g Protein: 3gFat: 1g

14. Brussels Sprouts

Preparation Time: 5 minutes
Cooking Time: 10 minutes
Servings: 4
INGREDIENTS:
- Almonds sliced: 1/4 cup
- Brussel sprouts: 2 cups
- Kosher salt
- Parmesan cheese: 1/4 cup grated
- Olive oil: 2 Tablespoons
- Everything bagel seasoning: 2 Tablespoons

DIRECTIONS:
1. In a saucepan, add Brussel sprouts with two cups of water and let it cook over medium flame for almost ten minutes.
2. Strain sprouts and cut them in half.
3. In a mixing bowl, add sliced brussels sprout with crushed almonds, oil, salt, parmesan cheese, and everything bagel seasoning.
4. Completely coat the sprouts.
5. Cook in the air fryer for 12-15 minutes at 375 F or until light brown.
6. Serve hot.

NUTRITION: Calories: 155 Carbohydrates: 3g Protein: 6g Fat: 3g

15. Vegetable Spring Rolls

Preparation Time: 10 minutes
Cooking Time: 15 minutes
Servings: 4
INGREDIENTS:

- Toasted sesame seeds
- Large carrots – grated
- Spring roll wrappers
- One egg white
- Gluten-free soy sauce, a dash
- Half cabbage: sliced
- Olive oil: 2 tbsp.

DIRECTIONS:

1. In a pan over high flame heat, 2 tbsp of oil and sauté the chopped vegetables. Then add soy sauce. Do not overcook the vegetables.
2. Turn off the heat and add toasted sesame seeds.
3. Lay spring roll wrappers flat on a surface and add egg white with a brush on the sides.
4. Add some vegetable mix in the wrapper and fold.
5. Spray oil in spring rolls and air fry for 8 minutes at 200 C.
6. Serve with dipping sauce.

NUTRITION: Calories 129 Fat 16.3g Carbohydrates 8.2g Protein 12.1 g

16. Avocado Fries

Preparation Time: 10 minutes
Cooking Time: 10 minutes
Servings: 2
INGREDIENTS:

- One avocado
- One egg
- Whole wheat breadcrumbs: 1/2 cup
- Salt: 1/2 teaspoon

DIRECTIONS:

1. Avocado should be firm and firm. Cut into wedges.
2. In a bowl, beat the egg with salt. In another bowl, add the crumbs.

3. Coat wedges in egg, then in crumbs.
4. Air fry them at 400 F for 8-10 minutes. Toss halfway through.
5. Serve hot.

NUTRITION: Calories: 251 Carbohydrates: 19g Protein: 6g Fat: 17g

17. Roasted Pumpkin

Preparation Time: 10 minutes
Cooking Time: 12 minutes
Servings: 4
INGREDIENTS:

- 1 1/2 lb. Pumpkin Deseeded & Chopped Roughly
- 3 Cloves Garlic, Minced
- 1 Tablespoon Olive Oil
- 1/8 Teaspoon Brown Sugar
- 1/8 Teaspoon Nutmeg, Ground
- 1/8 Teaspoon Cinnamon, Ground
- 1/8 Teaspoon Sea Salt, Fine

DIRECTIONS:

1. Place all of your ingredients in your air fryer basket, making sure that your pumpkin is coated well.
2. Cook at 370 F for 12 minutes.
3. Serve immediately.

NUTRITION: Calories: 260 Fat: 9g Carbs: 38g Protein: 9g

18. Herb Tomatoes

Preparation Time: 10 minutes
Cooking Time: 15 minutes
Servings: 4
INGREDIENTS:

- 4 Tomatoes, Big, Halved & Insides Removed
- 1/8 Teaspoon Sea Salt, Fine
- 1/8 Teaspoon Black Pepper
- 1 Tablespoon Olive Oil
- 2 Cloves Garlic, Minced
- 1/2 Teaspoon Thyme, Fresh & Chopped

DIRECTIONS:

1. Mix your tomatoes with salt, pepper, garlic, thyme, and oil.
2. Toss well and heat your air fryer to 390 F.
3. Cook for fifteen minutes and serve warm.

NUTRITION: Calories: 112 Fat: 1g Carbs: 4g
Protein: 4g

19. Roasted Parsnips

Preparation Time: 10 minutes
Cooking Time: 40 minutes
Servings: 6
INGREDIENTS:
- 2 lbs. Parsnips, Peeled & Cut into Chunks
- 2 Tablespoons Maple Syrup
- 1 Tablespoon Olive Oil
- 1 Tablespoon Parsley Flakes

DIRECTIONS:
1. Start by heating your air fryer to 360, and then add in your ingredients.
2. Make sure that your parsnips are well coated.
3. Cook for forty minutes, and then serve warm.

NUTRITION: Calories: 232 Fat: 7g Carbs: 41g
Protein: 3g

20. Honey Roasted Carrots

Preparation Time: 10 minutes
Cooking Time: 12 minutes
Servings: 4
INGREDIENTS:
- 1 Tablespoon Honey, Raw
- 3 Cups Baby Carrots
- 1 Tablespoon Olive Oil
- Sea Salt & Black Pepper to Taste

DIRECTIONS:
1. Put all ingredients into a bowl. Mix well.
2. Prepare your air fryer to 390 F.
3. Cook for 12 minutes.
4. Serve warm.

NUTRITION: Calories: 204 Fat: 10g Carbs: 29g
Protein: 1g

21. Herb Vegetables

Preparation Time: 10 minutes
Cooking Time: 18 minutes
Servings: 4
INGREDIENTS:
- 1 Red Bell Pepper, Sliced
- 8 Ounces Mushrooms, Sliced
- 1 cup Green Beans
- 3 Cloves Garlic, Sliced
- 1/3 Cup Red Onion, Diced
- 1 Teaspoon Olive Oil
- 1/2 Teaspoon Basil
- 1/2 Teaspoon Tarragon

DIRECTIONS:
1. Chopped green beans into two-inch pieces
2. Get out a bowl and mix your red onion, red bell pepper, mushrooms, garlic, and green beans.
3. Drizzle your olive oil next, making sure everything is mixed and coasted. Add in your herbs and toss again.
4. Place them in your air fryer basket, and roast until tender. This will take fourteen to eighteen minutes.
5. Serve warm.

NUTRITION: Calories: 44 Fat: 2g Carbs: 5g
Protein: 2.5g

22. Crisp Broccoli

Preparation Time: 10 minutes
Cooking Time: 14 minutes
Servings: 4
INGREDIENTS:
- 1 Tablespoon Lemon Juice, Fresh
- 2 Teaspoon Olive Oil
- 1 Head Broccoli

DIRECTIONS:
1. Start by rinsing your broccoli and patting it dry.
2. Cut it into florets, and then separate them. Make sure that if you use the stems, it's cut into one-inch chunks and peeled.
3. Toss your broccoli pieces with your lemon juice and olive oil until they're well coated.
4. Roast your broccoli in batches for ten for fourteen minutes each. They should be tender and crisp.
5. Serve warm.

NUTRITION: Calories: 90 Fat: 0.5g Carbs: 7g
Protein: 9g

23. Roasted Bell Pepper

Preparation Time: 10 minutes
Cooking Time: 20 minutes

Servings: 4

INGREDIENTS:

- 1 Teaspoon Olive Oil
- 1/2 Teaspoon Thyme
- 4 Cloves Garlic, Minced
- 4 Bell Peppers, Cut into Fourths

DIRECTIONS:

1. Start by putting your peppers in your basket and drizzling them with olive oil. Make sure they're coated well and then roast for fifteen minutes.
2. Sprinkle with thyme and garlic, roasting for an additional three to five minutes. They should be tender and serve warm.

NUTRITION: Calories: 74 Fat: 4g Carbs: 9g Protein: 1g

24. Garlic Asparagus

Preparation Time: 10 minutes
Cooking Time: 11 minutes
Servings: 4
INGREDIENTS:

- 1 lb. Asparagus, Rinsed & Trimmed
- 2 Teaspoons Olive Oil
- 3 Cloves Garlic, Minced
- 2 Tablespoons Balsamic Vinegar
- 1/2 Teaspoon Thyme

DIRECTIONS:

1. Start by getting out a large bowl to toss your asparagus in olive oil before placing your vegetables in the basket.
2. Sprinkle with garlic before roasting for eight to eleven minutes. Your asparagus should be tender but crisp.
3. Drizzle with thyme and balsamic vinegar before serving warm.

NUTRITION: Calories: 48 Fat: 2g Carbs: 6g Protein: 3g

25. Salmon Spring Rolls

Preparation Time: 15 minutes
Cooking Time: 20 minutes
Servings: 4
INGREDIENTS:

- 1/2 lb. Salmon Fillet
- 1 Teaspoon Toasted Sesame Oil
- 1 Onion, Sliced

- Rice Pepper Wrappers
- 1 Yellow Bell Pepper, Sliced Thin
- 1 Carrot, Shredded
- 1/3 Cup Flat Leaf Parsley, Chopped
- 1/4 Cup Basil, Fresh & Chopped

DIRECTIONS:

1. Start by placing your salmon in the air fryer, drizzling it with sesame oil, and add in your onion.
2. Cook for eight to ten minutes. Your onion should be tender, and the salmon should flake easily.
3. While this is cooking, get out a shallow bowl and fill it with warm water.
4. Dip your rice paper wrappers in one at a time. Make sure to place them on a clean work surface.
5. Top each wrapper with a bit of the salmon and onion mixture, bell pepper, carrot, basil, and parsley. Roll the wrappers up, making sure to close them.
6. Air fry at 380 F for seven to eight minutes. Cut in half before serving warm.

NUTRITION: Calories: 95 Fat: 2g Carbs: 8g Protein: 13g

26. Baby Potatoes

Preparation Time:
Cooking Time:
Servings:
Ingredients:
Servings: 2
Time: 15 Minutes
Calories: 94
Protein: 3.3 Grams
Fat: 2.5 Grams
Carbs: 15.9 Grams
INGREDIENTS:

- 250 Grams Baby Potatoes, Halved
- 1 Teaspoon Olive Oil
- 1/4 Teaspoon Oregano Powder
- 1/8 Teaspoon Garlic Powder
- 1/8 Teaspoon Thyme
- 1/8 Teaspoon Sea Salt, Fine
- 1/8 Teaspoon Black Pepper

DIRECTIONS:

1. Start by heating your air fryer to 350, and then wash and half your baby potatoes.

2. Toss these halves in olive oil, garlic powder, oregano, salt, pepper, and thyme.
3. Place them on a baking sheet accessory, roasting in your air fryer for thirty minutes.
4. You'll need to shake in about five minutes to make sure that all parts are exposed and will become crisp.
5. Serve warm.

NUTRITION: Calories: 68 Fat: 0.3g Carbs: 14g Protein: 1g

27. Curried Brussels Sprouts

Preparation Time: 10 minutes
Cooking Time: 20 minutes
Servings: 4
INGREDIENTS:

- 1 lb. Brussel Sprouts, end Trimmed & Halved
- 2 Teaspoons Olive Oil
- 1 Tablespoon Lemon Juice, Fresh
- 3 Teaspoons Curry Powder, Divided

DIRECTIONS:

1. Start by getting gout in a large bowl and mix your olive oil with a teaspoon of curry powder.
2. Toss your Brussel sprouts in, mixing until well coated. Place them in your air fryer basket, roasting for twelve minutes.
3. During this cooking time, you'll need to shake your basket once.
4. Sprinkle with the remaining curry powder and lemon juice, shaking your basket again.
5. Roast for an additional three to five minutes.
6. Your Brussel sprouts should be crisp and browned. Serve warm.

NUTRITION: Calories: 57 Fat: 1g Carbs: 8g Protein: 2g

28. Creamy Potatoes

Preparation time: 5 minutes
Cooking time: 20 minutes
Servings: 4
INGREDIENTS:

- 2 gold potatoes, cut into medium pieces
- 1 tablespoon olive oil
- Salt and black pepper to taste

- 2 tablespoons sour cream

DIRECTIONS:

1. In a baking dish that fits your air fryer, mix all the ingredients and toss.
2. Place the dish in the air fryer and cook at 370 degrees F for 20 minutes.
3. Divide between plates and serve as a side dish.

NUTRITION: Calories 201 Fat 8g Carbs 18g Protein 5g

29. Mint-Butter Stuffed Mushrooms

Preparation Time: 5 minutes
Cooking Time: 12 minutes
Servings: 3
INGREDIENTS

- 2 garlic cloves, minced
- 1 teaspoon ground black pepper
- 1/3 cup seasoned breadcrumbs
- 1 1/2 tablespoons fresh mint, chopped
- 1 teaspoon salt, or more to taste
- 1 1/2 tablespoons melted butter
- 14 medium-sized mushrooms, cleaned, stalks removed

DIRECTIONS

1. Mix all of the above ingredients, minus the mushrooms, in a mixing bowl to prepare the filling.
2. Then, stuff the mushrooms with the prepared filling.
3. Air-fry stuffed mushrooms at 375 degrees F for about 12 minutes.
4. Taste for doneness and serve at room temperature as a vegetarian appetizer.

NUTRITION: 290 Calories 14.7g Fat 13.4g Carbs 28g Protein

30. Ricotta and Leafy Green Omelet

Preparation Time: 5 minutes
Cooking Time: 15 minutes
Servings: 2
INGREDIENTS

- 1/3 cup Ricotta cheese
- 2 eggs, beaten

- 1/2 seeded and sliced red bell pepper
- 1 cup mixed greens, roughly chopped
- 1/2 green bell pepper, seeded and sliced
- 1/2 teaspoon dried basil
- 1/2 chipotle pepper, finely minced
- 1/2 teaspoon dried oregano

DIRECTIONS
1. Put some cooking spray inside of a baking dish.
2. Then, throw all ingredients into the baking dish; give it a good stir.
3. Bake at 325 degrees F for 15 minutes.

NUTRITION: Calories: 361 Fat: 20g Carbs: 21g Protein: 22g

31. Mayo Brussels Sprouts

Preparation time: 5 minutes
Cooking time: 15 minutes
Servings: 4
INGREDIENTS:

- 1-pound Brussels sprouts, trimmed and halved
- Salt and black pepper to taste
- 2 teaspoons olive oil
- 1/2 cup mayonnaise
- 2 tablespoons garlic, minced

DIRECTIONS:
1. In your air fryer, mix the sprouts, salt, pepper, and oil; toss well.
2. Cook the sprouts at 390 degrees F for 15 minutes.
3. Transfer them to a bowl; then add the mayonnaise and the garlic and toss.
4. Divide between plates and serve as a side dish.

NUTRITION: Calories 202 Fat 6g Carbs 12g Protein 8g

32. Pantano Romanesco with Goat Cheese

Preparation Time: 6 minutes
Cooking Time: 14 minutes
Servings: 4
INGREDIENTS

- 2 ounces goat cheese, sliced
- 2 shallots, thinly sliced

- 2 Pantano Romanesco tomatoes, cut into 1/2-inch slices
- 1 1/2 tablespoons extra-virgin olive oil
- 3/4 teaspoon sea salt
- 1 Fresh parsley, for garnish
- 1 Fresh basil, chopped

DIRECTIONS
1. Turn on the air fryer to 380 degrees F.
2. Now, pat each tomato slice dry using a paper towel. Sprinkle each slice with salt and chopped basil. Top with a slice of goat cheese.
3. Top with the shallot slices; drizzle with olive oil. Add the prepared tomato and feta bites to the air fryer food basket.
4. Cook in the air fryer for about 14 minutes.
5. Lastly, adjust seasonings to taste and serve garnished with fresh parsley leaves. Enjoy!

NUTRITION: Calories: 237 Fat: 20.4g Carbs: 0.9g Protein: 13g

33. Swiss Chard and Cheese Omelet

Preparation Time: 7 minutes
Cooking Time: 18 minutes
Servings: 2
INGREDIENTS

- 1 teaspoon garlic paste
- 1 1/2 tablespoons olive oil
- 1/2 cup crème fraiche
- 1/3 teaspoon ground black pepper, to your liking
- 1/3 cup Swiss cheese, crumbled
- 1 teaspoon cayenne pepper
- 1/3 cup Swiss chard, torn into pieces
- 2 eggs
- 1/4 cup yellow onions, chopped
- 1 teaspoon fine sea salt

DIRECTIONS
1. Crack your eggs into a mixing dish; then, add the crème fraiche, salt, ground black pepper, and cayenne pepper.
2. Glaze inside of a baking dish with olive oil and tilt it to spread evenly.
3. Scrape the egg/cream mixture into the baking dish. Add the other ingredients; mix to combine well.

4. Bake for 18 minutes at 292 degrees F.
5. Serve immediately.

NUTRITION: Calories: 146 Fat: 11g Carbs: 4g Protein: 9g

34. Mom's Jacket Potatoes

Preparation Time: 5 minutes
Cooking Time: 20 minutes
Servings: 4
INGREDIENTS
- 1/3 cup Cottage cheese, softened
- 1/3 cup Parmigiano-Reggiano cheese, grated
- 1 teaspoon black pepper
- 1 1/2 heaping tablespoons roughly chopped cilantro leaves
- 1/3 cup green onions, finely chopped
- 4 average-sized potatoes
- 2 1/2 tablespoons softened butter
- 1 teaspoon salt

DIRECTIONS
1. Firstly, stab your potatoes with a fork. Cook them in the air fryer basket for 20 minutes at 345 degrees F.
2. While the potatoes are cooking, make the filling by mixing the rest of the above ingredients.
3. Afterward, open the potatoes up and stuff them with the prepared filling. Bon appétit!

NUTRITION: Calories: 270 Fat: 10.9g Carbs: 35.2g Protein: 8.8g

35. Green Beans and Shallots

Preparation time: 5 minutes
Cooking time: 25 minutes
Servings: 4
INGREDIENTS:
- 1 1/2 pounds green beans, trimmed
- Salt and black pepper to taste
- 1/2-pound shallots, chopped
- 1/4 cup walnuts, chopped
- 2 tablespoons olive oil

DIRECTIONS:
1. In your air fryer, mix all ingredients and toss.
2. Cook for 25 minutes at 350 degrees F.

3. Divide between plates and serve as a side dish.

NUTRITION: Calories 182 Fat 3g Carbs 11g Protein 5g

36. Italian Mushroom Mix

Preparation time: 5 minutes
Cooking time: 15 minutes
Servings: 4
INGREDIENTS:
- 1-pound button mushrooms, halved
- 2 tablespoons parmesan cheese, grated
- 1 teaspoon Italian seasoning
- A pinch of salt and black pepper
- 2 tablespoons butter, melted

DIRECTION:
1. Mix together all the ingredients in a pan that fits the fryer and toss.
2. Position pan in the air fryer and cook at 360 degrees F for 15 minutes.
3. Divide the mix between plates and serve.

NUTRITION: Calories 194 Fat 4g Carbs 14g Protein 7g

37. Herbed Roasted Potatoes

Preparation Time: 5 minutes
Cooking Time: 17 minutes
Servings: 4
INGREDIENTS
- 1 teaspoon crushed dried thyme
- 1 teaspoon ground black pepper
- 2 tablespoons olive oil
- 1/2 tablespoon crushed dried rosemary
- 4 potatoes, peeled, washed, and cut into wedges
- 1/2 teaspoon seasoned salt

DIRECTIONS
1. Lay the potatoes in the air fryer cooking basket, drizzle olive oil over your potatoes.
2. Then, cook for 17 minutes at 353 degrees F.
3. Toss with the seasonings and serve warm with your favorite salad on the side.

NUTRITION: 208 Calories: 7.1g Fat: 33.8g Carbs: 3.6g Protein:

38. Easy Frizzled Leeks

Preparation Time: 25 minutes
Cooking Time: 18 minutes
Servings: 6
INGREDIENTS

- 1/2 teaspoon porcini powder
- 1 1/2 cup rice flour
- 1 tablespoon vegetable oil
- 2 medium-sized leeks, slice into julienne strips
- 2 large-sized dishes with ice water
- 2 teaspoons onion powder
- Fine sea salt, to taste
- Cayenne pepper, to taste

DIRECTIONS

1. Allow the leeks to soak in ice water for about 25 minutes; drain well.
2. Place the rice flour, salt, cayenne pepper, onions powder, and porcini powder into a resealable bag. Add the celery and shake to coat well.
3. Drizzle vegetable oil over the seasoned leeks. Air fry for 18 minutes with 390 degrees F for temperature; turn them mid through the cooking time.
4. Serve with homemade mayonnaise or any other sauce for dipping. Enjoy!

NUTRITION: 291 Calories: 6g Fat: 53.3g Carbs: 5.7g Protein:

39. Oyster Mushroom and Lemongrass Omelet

Preparation Time: 7 minutes
Cooking Time: 35 minutes
Servings: 2
INGREDIENTS

- 2 king oyster mushrooms, thinly sliced
- 1 lemongrass, chopped
- 1/2 teaspoon dried marjoram
- 2 eggs
- 1/3 cup Swiss cheese, grated
- 2 tablespoons sour cream
- 1 1/2 teaspoon dried rosemary
- 2 teaspoons red pepper flakes, crushed
- 2 tablespoons butter, melted

- 1/2 red onion
- 1/2 teaspoon garlic powder
- 1 teaspoon dried dill weed
- Sea salt
- Ground black pepper, to your liking

DIRECTIONS

1. Get the onion then peeled and sliced into thin rounds
2. Melt the margarine in a skillet that is placed over a medium flame. Then, sweat the onion, mushrooms, and lemongrass until they have softened, reserve.
3. Then, preheat the air fryer to 325 degrees F. Break eggs into a mixing bowl and whisk them well. Then, fold in the sour cream and give it a good stir.
4. Now, stir in the salt, black pepper, red pepper, rosemary, garlic powder, marjoram, and dill.
5. Grease the inside of an air fryer baking dish with a thin layer of a cooking spray.
6. Pour the egg/seasoning mixture into the baking dish; throw in the reserved mixture. Top with the Swiss cheese.
7. Set the timer for 35 minutes; cook until a knife inserted in the center comes out clean and dry.

NUTRITION: Calories: 200 Fat: 3g Carbs: 8g Protein: 30g

40. Spinach and Cheese Stuffed Baked Potatoes

Preparation Time: 15 minutes
Cooking Time: 20 minutes
Servings: 4
INGREDIENTS

- tablespoons extra-virgin olive oil
- 2/3 cup sour cream
- 11/2 cup baby spinach leaves, torn into small pieces
- pounds russet potatoes
- 2 garlic cloves, peeled and finely minced
- 1/4 teaspoon fine sea salt
- 1/4 teaspoon black pepper (cracked), or to taste
- 1/3 cup Cheddar cheese, freshly grated

DIRECTIONS

1. Firstly, stab the potatoes with a fork.
2. Preheat the air fryer to 345 degrees F. Now, cook the potatoes for 14 minutes.
3. Meanwhile, make the filling by mixing the rest of the above items.
4. Afterward that, open the potatoes up and stuff them with the prepared filling. Bon appétit!

NUTRITION: 327 Calories: 7g Fat: 59g Carbs: 9.4g Protein

DIABETICS AIR FRYER FISH AND SEAFOOD

41. Crispy Fish Sandwiches

Preparation Time: 10 minutes
Cooking Time: 10 minutes
Servings: 2
INGREDIENTS:

- 2 fillets Cod
- 2 tablespoons All-purpose flour
- 1/4 teaspoon Pepper
- 1 tablespoon Lemon juice
- 1/4 teaspoon Salt
- 1/2 teaspoon Garlic powder
- 1 egg
- 1/2 tablespoon Mayo
- 1/2 cup Whole wheat breadcrumbs

DIRECTIONS:

1. In a bowl, add salt, flour, pepper, and garlic powder.
2. In a separate bowl, add lemon juice, mayo, and egg.
3. In another bowl, add the breadcrumbs.
4. Coat the fish in flour, then in egg, then in breadcrumbs.
5. With cooking oil, spray the basket and put the fish in the basket. Also, spray the fish with cooking oil.
6. Cook at 400 F for ten minutes. This fish is soft, be careful if you flip.

NUTRITION: Calories 218 Carbs: 7g Fat: 12g Protein: 22g

42. Breaded Hake With Green Chili Pepper And Mayonnaise

Preparation Time: 15 minutes
Cooking Time: 30 minutes
Servings: 4
INGREDIENTS:

- 4 breaded hake fillets
- 8 tsps. Mayonnaise
- Green mojito
- 8 tsps. Extra virgin olive oil

DIRECTIONS:

1. Paint the breaded hake fillets with extra virgin olive oil.
2. Prepare air fryer and put in the basket. Cook at 180 C for 30 minutes.
3. Meanwhile, put in a bowl 8 teaspoons of mayonnaise and 2 of green mojito.
4. Serve the breaded hake fillets with the green mojito mayonnaise.

NUTRITION: Calories: 132 Fat: 4.38g Carbs: 0.41g Protein: 21.38g

43. Salmon With Brown Sugar Glaze

Preparation Time: 10 minutes
Cooking Time: 15 minutes
Servings: 1
INGREDIENTS:

- 2 tbsps. Dijon mustard
- 4 (6 oz.) Boneless salmon fillets
- 1/4 Cup light brown sugar
- Salt
- Ground black pepper

DIRECTIONS:

1. Change temperature of the Air Fryer to 375F.
2. Sprinkle the Fryer basket with cooking spray.
3. Apply pepper and salt on the fish then place it in the Air Fryer basket.
4. In a separate small bowl, whisk together brown sugar and Dijon mustard.
5. Coat the fish properly with the mixture.
6. Cook for about 15 minutes.
7. Serve

NUTRITION: Calories: 553 Fat: 9.2g Carbs: 18.3g Protein: 28.9g

44. Catfish With Green Beans

Preparation Time: 15 minutes
Cooking Time: 20 minutes
Servings: 2
INGREDIENTS:

- Catfish fillets: 2 pieces

- Green beans: half cup, trimmed
- Honey: 2 teaspoons
- Freshly ground black pepper
- Salt, to taste
- Crushed red pepper: half tsp.
- Flour: 1/4 cup
- One egg, lightly beaten
- Dill pickle relish: 3/4 teaspoon
- Apple cider vinegar: half tsp
- 1/3 cup whole-wheat breadcrumbs
- Mayonnaise: 2 tablespoons
- Dill
- Lemon wedges

DIRECTIONS:

1. In a bowl, add green beans, spray them with cooking oil. Coat with crushed red pepper, 1/8 teaspoon of kosher salt, and half tsp. of honey.
2. Cook in the air fryer at 400 F until soft and browned, for 12 minutes. Take out from fryer and cover with aluminum foil
3. IN the meantime, coat catfish in flour. Then dip in egg to coat, then in breadcrumbs. Place fish in an air fryer basket and spray with cooking oil.
4. Prepare at 400 F and cook for 8 minutes, until cooked through and golden brown.
5. Sprinkle with pepper and salt. In the meantime, mix vinegar, dill, relish, mayonnaise, and honey in a bowl. Serve the sauce with fish and green beans.

NUTRITION: Calories 243 Fat 18 g Carbs 18 g Protein 33 g

45. Honey-glazed Salmon

Preparation Time: 10 minutes
Cooking Time: 15 minutes
Servings: 2
INGREDIENTS:

- Gluten-free Soy Sauce: 6 tsp
- Salmon Fillets: 2 pcs
- Sweet rice wine: 3 tsp
- Water: 1 tsp
- Honey: 6 tbsp.

Directions:

1. In a bowl, mix sweet rice wine, soy sauce, honey, and water.

2. Set half of it aside.
3. In the half of it, marinate the fish and let it rest for two hours.
4. Let the air fryer preheat to 180 C
5. Cook the fish for 8 minutes, flip halfway through and cook for another five minutes.
6. Baste the salmon with marinade mixture after 3 or 4 minutes.
7. The half of marinade, pour in a saucepan reduce to half, serve with a sauce.

NUTRITION: Calories 254 Carbs 9.9 g Fat 12 g Protein 20 g

46. Grilled Salmon With Lemon

Preparation Time: 2 hours
Cooking Time: 10 minutes
Servings: 4
INGREDIENTS:

- Olive oil: 2 tablespoons
- 2 Salmon fillets
- Lemon juice
- Water: 1/3 cup
- Gluten-free light soy sauce: 1/3 cup
- Honey: 1/3 cup
- Scallion slices
- Cherry tomato
- Freshly ground black pepper, garlic powder, kosher salt to taste

DIRECTIONS:

1. Season salmon with pepper and salt
2. In a bowl, mix honey, soy sauce, lemon juice, water, oil. Add salmon in this marinade and let it rest for least two hours.
3. Let the air fryer preheat at 180°C
4. Put and cook the fish in the air fryer and for 8 minutes.
5. Move to a dish and top with scallion slices.

NUTRITION: Cal 211 Fat 9g Protein 15g Carbs 4.9g

47. Sesame Seeds Coated Tuna

Preparation Time: 10 minutes
Cooking Time: 10 minutes
Servings: 2

INGREDIENTS:

- 1 egg white
- 1/4 cup white sesame seeds
- 1 tbsp. black sesame seeds
- Salt and ground black pepper
- 6-oz. tuna steaks

DIRECTIONS:

1. Get a shallow bowl, beat the egg white.
2. In another bowl, mix the sesame seeds, salt, and black pepper.
3. Dip the tuna steaks into the egg white and then coat with the sesame seeds mixture.
4. Press the "power button" of air fry oven and turn the dial to select the "air fry" mode.
5. Press the time button and set the cooking time to 6 minutes.
6. Now push the temp button and rotate the dial to set the temperature at 400°F.
7. Press the "start/pause" button to start.
8. When the unit beeps to show that it is preheated, open the lid.
9. Arrange the tuna steaks in greased "air fry basket" and insert in the oven.
10. Flip the tuna steaks once halfway through.
11. Serve hot.

NUTRITION: Calories: 450 kcal; Fat: 21.9g; Carbs: 5.4g; Protein: 56.7g

48. Salmon Cakes

Preparation Time:
Cooking Time: 10 minutes
Servings: 2
INGREDIENTS:

- Fresh salmon fillet 8 oz.
- Egg 1
- Salt 1/8 tsp
- Garlic powder 1/4 tsp
- Sliced lemon 1

DIRECTIONS:

1. In the bowl, chop the salmon, add the egg & spices.
2. Form tiny cakes.
3. Let the Air fryer preheat to 390 F. On the bottom of the air fryer bowl lay sliced lemons—place cakes on top.

4. Cook them for seven minutes. Based on your diet preferences, eat with your chosen dip.

NUTRITION: Calories: 194 Fat: 9g Carbs: 1g Protein: 25g

49. Crumbed Fish

Preparation Time: 10 minutes
Cooking Time: 12 minutes
Servings: 2
INGREDIENTS:

- 1 mug completely dry breadcrumbs
- 1/4 mug vegetable oil
- 4 go to pieces fillets
- 1 beaten egg
- 1 sliced lemon.

DIRECTIONS:

1. Preheat an air fryer to 351°F.
2. Mix breadcrumbs and oil with each other in a dish. Mix up until blend comes to be loosened as well as crumbly.
3. Dip fish fillets right into the egg; shake off any type of unwanted. Dip fillets into the bread crumb mix; layer uniformly as well as completely.
4. Lay coated fillets carefully in the preheated air fryer. Prepare up until fish flakes quickly with a fork, about 12 mins.
5. Garnish with lemon pieces.

NUTRITION: Calories: 148 Carbs: 13.8g Fat: 6.7g Protein: 7.2g

50. Shrimp With Delicious Sauce

Preparation Time: 10 minutes
Cooking Time: 20 minutes
Servings: 4
INGREDIENTS:

- Whole wheat breadcrumbs: 3/4 cup
- Raw shrimp: 4 cups, deveined, peeled
- Flour: half cup
- Paprika: one tsp
- Chicken Seasoning, to taste
- 2 tbsp. of one egg white
- Kosher salt and pepper to taste
- Sauce

- Sweet chili sauce: 1/4 cup
- Plain Greek yogurt: 1/3 cup
- Sriracha: 2 tbsp.

DIRECTIONS:
1. Let the Air Fryer preheat to 400 degrees F.
2. Add the seasonings to shrimp and coat well.
3. In three separate bowls, add flour, breadcrumbs, and egg whites.
4. First coat the shrimp in flour, dab lightly in egg whites, then in the breadcrumbs.
5. With cooking oil, spray the shrimp.
6. Place the shrimps in an air fryer, cook for four minutes, turn the shrimp over, and cook for another four minutes. Serve with micro green and sauce.
7. Sauce: Mix all ingredients in a bowl. And serve.

NUTRITION: Calories 229 Fat 10g Carbohydrates 13g Protein 22g.

51. Shrimp Scampi

Preparation Time: 10 minutes
Cooking Time: 12 minutes
Servings: 4
INGREDIENTS:
- 1-pound shrimp, peeled, deveined
- 1 tablespoon minced garlic
- 1 tablespoon minced basil
- 1 tablespoon lemon juice
- 1 teaspoon dried chives
- 1 teaspoon dried basil
- 2 teaspoons red pepper flakes
- 4 tablespoons butter, unsalted
- 2 tablespoons chicken stock

DIRECTIONS:
1. Switch on the air fryer, insert fryer pan, grease it with olive oil, then shut with its lid, set the fryer at 330 degrees F, and preheat for 5 minutes.
2. Add butter in it and red pepper and garlic and cook for 2 minutes or until the butter has melted.
3. Then add remaining ingredients in the pan, stir until mixed and continue cooking for 5 minutes until shrimps have cooked, stirring halfway through.

4. When done, remove the pan from the air fryer, stir the shrimp scampi, let it rest for 1 minute and then stir again.
5. Garnish shrimps with basil leaves and serve.

NUTRITION: Calories: 221 Carbs: 1 g Fat: 13 g Protein: 23 g

52. Sesame Seeds Fish Fillet

Preparation Time: 10 minutes
Cooking Time: 20 minutes
Servings: 2
INGREDIENTS:
- Plain flour: 3 tablespoons
- One egg, beaten
- 5 frozen fish fillets
- Oil: 2 tablespoons
- Sesame seeds: 1/2 cup
- Rosemary herbs
- 5-6 biscuit's crumbs
- Kosher salt& pepper, to taste

DIRECTIONS:
1. For two-minute sauté the sesame seeds in a pan, without oil. Brown them and set it aside.
2. In a plate, mix all coating ingredients
3. Place the aluminum foil on the air fryer basket and let it preheat at 200 C.
4. First, coat the fish in flour. Then in egg, then in the coating mix.
5. Place in the Air fryer. If fillets are frozen, cook for ten minutes, then turn the fillet and cook for another four minutes.
6. If not frozen, then cook for eight minutes and two minutes.

NUTRITION: Cal 250 Fat: 8g Carbs: 12.4g Protein: 20g

53. Cajun Salmon

Preparation Time: 10 minutes
Cooking Time: 20 minutes
Servings: 1
INGREDIENTS:
- 1-piece Fresh salmon
- 2 tbsp. Cajun seasoning
- Lemon juice

DIRECTIONS:

1. Let the air fryer preheat to 180 C.
2. Pat dry the salmon fillet. Rub lemon juice and Cajun seasoning over the fish fillet.
3. Place in the air fryer, cook for 7 minutes.
4. Serve with salad greens and lime wedges.

NUTRITION: Cal 216 Fat 19g Carbohydrates 5.6g Protein 19.2g

54. Scallops With Creamy Tomato Sauce

Preparation Time: 10 minutes
Cooking Time: 10 minutes
Servings: 2
INGREDIENTS:

- Sea scallops eight jumbo
- Tomato Paste: 1 tbsp.
- Chopped fresh basil one tablespoon
- 3/4 cup of low-fat Whipping Cream
- Kosher salt half teaspoon
- Ground Freshly black pepper half teaspoon
- Minced garlic 1 teaspoon
- Frozen Spinach, thawed half cup
- Oil Spray

DIRECTIONS:

1. Take a seven-inch pan (heatproof) and add spinach in a single layer at the bottom
2. Rub olive oil on both sides of scallops, season with kosher salt and pepper.
3. On top of the spinach, place the seasoned scallops
4. Put the pan in the air fryer and cook for ten minutes at 350F, until scallops are cooked completely, and internal temperature reaches 135F.
5. Serve immediately.

NUTRITION: Calories: 259 Carbohydrates: 6g Protein: 19g Fat: 13g

55. Crab Cake

Preparation Time: 10 minutes
Cooking Time: 15 minutes
Servings: 2
INGREDIENTS:

- 8 ounces crab meat, wild-caught
- 2 tablespoons almond flour

- 1/4 cup red bell pepper, cored, chopped
- 2 green onion, chopped
- 1 teaspoon old bay seasoning
- 1 tablespoon Dijon mustard
- 2 tablespoons mayonnaise, reduced fat

DIRECTIONS:

1. Switch on the air fryer, insert fryer basket, grease it with olive oil, then shut with its lid, set the fryer at 370 degrees F, and preheat for 5 minutes.
2. Meanwhile, place all the ingredients in a bowl, stir until well combined and then shape the mixture into four patties.
3. Open the fryer, add crab patties in it, spray oil over the patties, close with its lid and cook for 10 minutes until nicely golden and crispy, flipping the patties halfway through the frying.
4. When air fryer beeps, open its lid, transfer the crab patties onto a serving plate and serve with lemon wedges.

NUTRITION: Calories: 123 Carbs: 5 g Fat: 6 g Protein: 12 g

56. Quick Paella

Preparation Time: 7 minutes
Cooking Time: 13 – 17 minutes
Servings: 4
INGREDIENTS:

- 1 (10-ounce) package frozen cooked rice, thawed
- 1 (6-ounce) jar artichoke hearts, drained and chopped
- 1/4 cup vegetable broth
- 1/2 teaspoon turmeric
- 1/2 teaspoon dried thyme
- 1 cup frozen cooked small shrimp
- 1/2 cup frozen baby peas
- 1 tomato, diced

DIRECTIONS:

1. In a 6-by-6-by-2-inch pan, combine the rice, artichoke hearts, vegetable broth, turmeric, and thyme, and stir gently.
2. Prepare and put in the air fryer. Cook for 9 minutes or until the rice is hot.
3. Remove from the air fryer and gently stir in the shrimp, peas, and tomato. Cook for 5

to 8 minutes or until the shrimp and peas are hot and the paella is bubbling.

NUTRITION: Calories: 345 Fat: 1g Carbohydrates: 66g Protein: 18g

57. Crab Ratatouille

Preparation Time: 15 minutes
Cooking Time: 11 minutes
Servings: 4
INGREDIENTS:
- 1 1/2 cups peeled, cubed eggplant
- 1 onion, chopped
- 1 red bell pepper, chopped
- 2 large tomatoes, chopped
- 1 tablespoon olive oil
- 1/2 teaspoon dried thyme
- 1/2 teaspoon dried basil
- Pinch salt
- Freshly ground black pepper
- 11/2 cups cooked crabmeat, picked over

DIRECTIONS:
1. Combine the eggplant, onion, bell pepper, tomatoes, olive oil, thyme, and basil in a 6-inch metal bowl. Sprinkle with salt and pepper.
2. Roast for 9 minutes, then remove the bowl from the air fryer and stir.
3. Add the crabmeat and roast for 2 to 5 minutes or until the ratatouille is bubbling and the vegetables are tender.
4. Serve immediately.

NUTRITION: Calories: 147 Fat: 5g Carbohydrates: 10g Protein: 16g

58. Seafood Tacos

Preparation Time: 15 minutes
Cooking Time: 9 -12 minutes
Servings: 2
INGREDIENTS:
- 1-pound white fish fillets, such as snapper
- 1 tablespoon olive oil
- 3 tablespoons lemon juice, divided
- 11/2 cups chopped red cabbage
- 1/2 cup salsa
- 1/3 cup sour cream
- 6 soft flour tortillas

- 2 avocados, peeled and chopped

DIRECTIONS:
1. Brush the fish with olive oil and sprinkle with 1 tablespoon of lemon juice.
2. Place in the air fryer basket and air-fry for 9 to 12 minutes or until the fish flakes when tested with a fork.
3. Meanwhile, combine the remaining 2 tablespoons of lemon juice, cabbage, salsa, and sour cream in a medium bowl.
4. When the fish is cooked, remove it from the air fryer basket and break it into large pieces.
5. Let everyone assemble their taco combining the fish, tortillas, cabbage mixture, and avocados.

NUTRITION: Calories: 491 Fat: 29g Carbohydrates: 29g Protein: 31g

59. Crispy Herbed Salmon

Preparation Time: 5 minutes
Cooking Time: 9 - 12 minutes
Servings: 4
INGREDIENTS:
- 4 (6-ounce) skinless salmon fillets
- 3 tablespoons honey mustard
- 1/2 teaspoon dried thyme
- 1/2 teaspoon dried basil
- 1/4 cup panko breadcrumbs
- 1/3 cup crushed potato chips
- 2 tablespoons olive oil

DIRECTIONS:
1. Place the salmon on a plate. Get a bowl, combine the mustard, thyme, and basil, and spread evenly over the salmon.
2. In another small bowl, combine the breadcrumbs and potato chips and mix well. Drizzle in the olive oil and mix until combined.
3. Place the salmon in the air fryer basket and gently but firmly press the bread crumb mixture onto the top of each fillet.
4. Cook until the salmon reaches at least 145F on a meat thermometer, and the topping is browned and crisp.

NUTRITION: Calories: 373 Fat: 21g Carbohydrates: 13g Protein: 34g

60. Asian Steamed Tuna

Preparation Time: 10 minutes
Cooking Time: 10 minutes
Servings: 4
INGREDIENTS:

- 4 small tuna steaks
- 2 tablespoons low-sodium soy sauce
- 2 teaspoons sesame oil
- 2 teaspoons rice wine vinegar
- 1 teaspoon grated fresh ginger
- 1/8 teaspoon pepper
- 1 stalk lemongrass, bent in half
- 3 tablespoons lemon juice

DIRECTIONS:

1. Place the tuna steaks on a plate.
2. Put the soy sauce, sesame oil, rice wine vinegar, ginger, and mix well in a small bowl.
3. Pour this mixture over the tuna and marinate for 10 minutes.
4. Rub the soy sauce mixture gently into both sides of the tuna. Sprinkle with pepper.
5. Place the lemongrass on the air fryer basket and top with the steaks. Put the lemon juice and 1 tablespoon water in the pan below the basket.
6. Cook fish for 10 minutes or until the tuna registers at least 145°F. Discard the lemongrass and serve the tuna.
7. Air Fryer tip: Keep an eye on the liquid in the pan below the air fryer basket when this recipe is cooking. The tuna will give off liquid as it cooks, and you don't want the pan to overflow.

NUTRITION: Calories: 292 Fat: 14 Carbohydrates: 1g Protein: 38g

61. Tuna Veggie Stir-Fry

Preparation Time: 15 minutes
Cooking Time: 7 - 12 minutes
Servings: 4
INGREDIENTS:

- 1 tablespoon olive oil
- 1 red bell pepper, chopped
- 1 cup green beans
- 1 onion, sliced

- 2 cloves garlic, sliced
- 2 tablespoons low-sodium soy sauce
- 1 tablespoon honey
- 1/2-pound fresh tuna, cubed

DIRECTIONS:

1. Cut green beans into 2-inch pieces
2. In a 6-inch metal bowl, combine the olive oil, pepper, green beans, onion, and garlic.
3. Cook in the air fryer for 4 to 6 minutes, stirring once, until crisp and tender. Add soy sauce, honey, and tuna, and stir.
4. Cook for another 3 to 6 minutes, stirring once until the tuna is cooked as desired. Tuna can be served rare or medium-rare, or you can cook it until well done.

NUTRITION: Calories: 187 Fat: 8g Carbohydrates: 12g Protein: 17g

62. Scallops and Spring Veggies

Preparation Time: 10 minutes
Cooking Time: 10 minutes
Servings: 4
INGREDIENTS:

- 1/2-pound asparagus ends trimmed, cut into 2-inch pieces
- 1 cup sugar snap peas
- 1-pound sea scallops
- 1 tablespoon lemon juice
- 2 teaspoons olive oil
- 1/2 teaspoon dried thyme
- Pinch salt
- Freshly ground black pepper

DIRECTIONS:.

1. Put asparagus and sugar snap peas in the air fryer basket.
2. Cook for 2 to 3 minutes or until the vegetables are just starting to get tender.
3. Meanwhile, check the scallops for a small muscle attached to the side, and pull it off and discard.
4. Put the scallops with lemon juice, olive oil, thyme, salt, and pepper in a bowl. Place into the air fryer basket on top of the vegetables.
5. Steam for 5 to 7 minutes, tossing the basket once during cooking time until the

scallops are just firm when tested with your finger and are opaque in the center, and the vegetables are tender.

6. Serve immediately.

NUTRITION: Calories: 162 Fat: 4g Carbohydrates: 10g Protein: 22g

63. Snapper Scampi

Preparation Time: 5 minutes
Cooking Time: 10 minutes
Servings: 4
INGREDIENTS:

- 4 (6-ounce) skinless snapper or arctic char fillets
- 1 tablespoon olive oil
- 3 tablespoons lemon juice, divided
- 1/2 teaspoon dried basil
- Pinch salt
- Freshly ground black pepper
- 2 tablespoons butter
- 2 cloves garlic, minced

DIRECTIONS:

1. Massage fish fillets with olive oil and 1 tablespoon of lemon juice. Sprinkle with the basil, salt, and pepper, and place in the air fryer basket.
2. Grill the fish for 7 to 8 minutes or until the fish just flakes when tested with a fork. Remove the fish from the basket and put it on a serving plate. Cover to keep warm.
3. In a 6-by-6-by-2-inch pan, combine the butter, remaining 2 tablespoons lemon juice, and garlic.
4. Cook in the air fryer for 1 to 2 minutes or until the garlic is sizzling.
5. Pour this mixture over the fish and serve.

NUTRITION: Calories: 265 Fat: 11g Carbohydrates: 1g Protein: 39g

64. Coconut Shrimp

Preparation Time: 15 minutes
Cooking Time: 5 - 7 minutes
Servings: 4
INGREDIENTS:

- 1 (8-ounce) can crushed pineapple
- 1/2 cup sour cream
- 1/4 cup pineapple preserves

- 2 egg whites
- 2/3 cup cornstarch
- 2/3 cup sweetened coconut
- 1 cup panko breadcrumbs
- 1-pound uncooked large shrimp, thawed if frozen, deveined, and shelled
- Olive oil for misting

DIRECTIONS:

1. Strain crushed pineapple well, reserving the juice.
2. Put pineapple, sour cream, and preserves in a bowl. Mix well. Set aside.
3. Whisk egg whites in a bowl then put 2 tablespoons of the pineapple liquid.
4. Prepare cornstarch on a plate. Put coconut and breadcrumbs on another plate.
5. Roll shrimp into the cornstarch, shake it off, then dip into the egg white mixture and finally into the coconut mixture.
6. Place the shrimp in the air fryer basket and mist with oil. Air-fry for 5 to 7 minutes or until the shrimp are crisp and golden brown.

NUTRITION: Calories 310 Fat: 16g Carbohydrates: 31g Protein: 9g

65. Fish and Chips

Preparation Time: 10 minutes
Cooking Time: 20 minutes
Servings: 4
INGREDIENTS:

- 4 (4-ounce) fish fillets
- Pinch salt
- Freshly ground black pepper
- 1/2 teaspoon dried thyme
- 1 egg white
- 3/4 cup crushed potato chips
- 2 tablespoons olive oil, divided
- 2 russet potatoes

DIRECTIONS:

1. Peeled and cut russet potatoes into strips
2. Dry fish fillets and sprinkle with salt, pepper, and thyme. Set aside.
3. In a shallow bowl, beat the egg white until foamy. In another bowl, combine the potato chips and 1 tablespoon of olive oil and mix until combined.

4. Dip the fish fillets into the egg white, then into the crushed potato chip mixture to coat.
5. Toss the fresh potato strips with the remaining 1 tablespoon olive oil.
6. Use your separator to divide the air fryer basket in half, then fry the chips and fish.
7. The chips will take about 20 minutes; the fish will take about 10 to 12 minutes to cook.

NUTRITION: Calories: 374 Fat: 16g Carbohydrates: 38g Protein: 30g

66. Parmesan Walnut Salmon

Preparation Time: 10 minutes
Cooking Time: 12 minutes
Servings: 4
INGREDIENTS:
- 4 salmon fillets
- 1/4 cup parmesan cheese, grated
- 1/2 cup walnuts
- 1 tsp olive oil
- 1 tbsp lemon rind

DIRECTIONS:
1. Preheat the air fryer to 370 F.
2. Spray an air fryer baking dish with cooking spray.
3. Place salmon on a baking dish.
4. Add walnuts into the food processor and process until finely ground.
5. Mix ground walnuts with parmesan cheese, oil, and lemon rind. Stir well.
6. Spoon walnut mixture over the salmon and press gently.
7. Cook for 12 minutes.
8. Serve and enjoy.

NUTRITION: Calories 420 Fat 27.4 g Carbohydrates 2 g Protein 46.3 g

67. Lemony and Spicy Coconut Crusted Salmon

Preparation Time: 10 minutes
Cooking Time: 6 minutes
Servings: 4
INGREDIENTS:
- 1pound salmon

- 1/2 cup flour
- 2 egg whites
- 1/2 cup breadcrumbs
- 1/2 cup unsweetened coconut, shredded
- 1/4 teaspoon lemon zest
- Salt
- Freshly ground black pepper
- 1/4 teaspoon cayenne pepper
- 1/4 teaspoon red pepper flakes, crushed
- Vegetable oil, as required

DIRECTIONS:
1. Ready the Air fryer to 400 degrees F and grease an Air fryer basket.
2. Mix the flour, salt, and black pepper in a dish.
3. Beat egg whites in a shallow dish.
4. Mix the breadcrumbs, coconut, lime zest, salt, and cayenne pepper in a third shallow dish.
5. Coat salmon in the flour, then dip in the egg whites and then into the breadcrumb mixture evenly.
6. Put salmon in the basket and drizzle with vegetable oil.
7. Cook for about 6 minutes and dish out to serve warm.

NUTRITION: Calories: 558 Fat: 22.2g Carbohydrates: 18.6g Protein: 43g

68. Salmon Jerky

Preparation Time: 2 hours
Cooking Time: 4 hours 5 minutes
Servings: 4
INGREDIENTS:
- 1 lb. salmon, skin and bones removed
- 1/4 cup of soy sauce
- 1/2 tsp. ground ginger
- 1/4 tsp. red pepper flakes
- 1/2 tsp. liquid smoke
- 1/4 tsp. ground black pepper
- Juice of 1/2 medium lime

DIRECTIONS:
1. Slice salmon into 1/4-inch-thick slices, 4inch long
2. Place strips into large storage bag or covered bowl and add remaining

ingredients. Allow marinating for 2 hours in the refrigerator.

3. Place each strip into the air fryer basket in single layer. Adjust the temperature to 140 Degrees F and set the timer for 4 hours.

4. Cool then store in sealed container until ready to eat.

NUTRITION: Calories: 108 Protein: 15.1g Fat: 4.1g Carbs: 1.0g

69. Hawaiian Salmon

Preparation Time: 10 minutes
Cooking Time: 10 minutes
Servings: 2
INGREDIENTS:
- 20-ounce canned pineapple pieces and juice
- 2 medium salmon fillets; boneless
- 1/2 tsp. ginger; grated
- 2 tsp. garlic powder
- 1 tsp. onion powder
- 1 tbsp. balsamic vinegar
- Salt and black pepper to the taste

DIRECTIONS:
1. Season salmon with garlic powder, onion powder, salt, and black pepper, rub well.
2. Transfer to heatproof dish that fits your air fryer, add ginger and pineapple chunks, and toss them gently
3. Drizzle the vinegar all over, put in your air fryer, and cook at 350degreesF for 10 minutes.
4. Divide everything among plates and serve

NUTRITION: Calories: 261 Fat: 12g Carbs: 8.5g Protein: 29g

70. Salmon Thyme and Parsley

Preparation Time: 10 minutes
Cooking Time: 12 minutes
Servings: 4
INGREDIENTS:
- 4 salmon fillets; boneless
- 4 thyme sprigs
- 4 parsley sprigs
- 3 tbsp. extra virgin olive oil

- 1 yellow onion; chopped
- 3 tomatoes; sliced
- Juice from 1 lemon
- Salt and black pepper to the taste

DIRECTIONS:
1. Drizzle 1 tablespoon oil in pan that fits your air fryer; add layer of tomatoes, salt, and pepper.
2. Drizzle 1 more tablespoon oil, add fish, season them with salt and pepper.
3. Drizzle the rest of the oil, add thyme and parsley springs, onions, lemon juice, salt and pepper, place in your air fryer's basket
4. Cook at 360degreesF for 12 minutes, shaking once.
5. Divide everything on plates and serve right away

NUTRITION: Calories: 469 Fat: 34g Carbs: 1.2g Protein: 36g

71. Miso Fish

Preparation Time: 10 minutes
Cooking Time: 10 minutes
Servings: 2
INGREDIENTS:
- 2 cod fish fillets
- 1 tbsp garlic, chopped
- 2 tsp swerve
- 2 tbsp miso

DIRECTIONS:
1. Add all ingredients to the Ziplock bag. Shake well place in the refrigerator overnight.
2. Place marinated fish fillets into the air fryer basket and cooked at 350 F for 10 minutes.
3. Serve and enjoy.

NUTRITION: Calories 229 Fat 2.6 g Carbohydrates 10.9 g, Protein 43.4 g

72. Tilapia Fish Fillets

Preparation Time: 10 minutes
Cooking Time: 7 minutes
Servings: 2
INGREDIENTS:
- 2 tilapia fillets
- 1 tsp old bay seasoning
- 1/2 tsp butter

- 1/4 tsp lemon pepper
- Pepper
- Salt

DIRECTIONS:
1. Spray air fryer basket with cooking spray.
2. Place fish fillets into the air fryer basket and season with lemon pepper, old bay seasoning, pepper, and salt.
3. Spray fish fillets with cooking spray and cook at 400 F for 7 minutes.
4. Serve and enjoy.

NUTRITION: Calories 80 Fat 2 g Carbohydrates 0.2 g Protein 15 g

73. Fish Sticks

Preparation Time: 10 minutes
Cooking Time: 25 minutes
Servings: 4
INGREDIENTS:

- 1 lb. cod fillet; cut into 3/4inch strips
- 1 oz. pork rinds, finely ground
- 1 large egg.
- 1/4 cup ground almond flour
- 1 tbsp. coconut oil
- 1/2 tsp. Old Bay seasoning

DIRECTIONS:
1. Put the ground pork rinds, almond flour, old bay seasoning, and coconut oil into large bowl and mix. Take medium bowl, whisk the egg
2. Soak each fish stick into the egg and slowly roll into the flour mixture. Make sure to coat evenly.
3. Arrange the fish sticks into the air fryer basket
4. Adjust the temperature to 400 Degrees F and set the timer for 10 minutes or until golden. Serve immediately.

NUTRITION: Calories: 205 Protein: 24.4g Fiber: 0.8g Fat: 10.7g Carbs: 1.6g

74. Lime Trout and Shallots

Preparation Time: 10 minutes
Cooking Time: 17 minutes
Servings: 4
INGREDIENTS:

- 4 trout fillets; boneless

- 3 garlic cloves; minced
- 6 shallots; chopped.
- 1/2 cup butter; melted
- 1/2 cup olive oil
- Juice of 1 lime
- A pinch of salt and black pepper

DIRECTIONS:
1. In pan that fits the air fryer, combine the fish with the shallots and the rest of the ingredients toss gently
2. Place the pan in the fryer and cook at 390degreesF for 12 minutes, flipping the fish halfway.
3. Arrange in the plates and serve with side salad.

NUTRITION: Calories: 270 Fat: 12g Carbs: 6g Protein: 12g

75. Trout and Zucchinis

Preparation Time: 5 minutes
Cooking Time: 15 minutes
Servings: 4
INGREDIENTS:

- 3 zucchinis, cut in medium chunks
- 4 trout fillets; boneless
- 1/4 cup tomato sauce
- 1 garlic clove; minced
- 1/2 cup cilantro; chopped.
- 1 tbsp. lemon juice
- 2 tbsp. olive oil
- Salt and black pepper to taste

DIRECTIONS:
1. In the pan that fits your air fryer mix the fish with the other ingredients.
2. Toss introduce in the fryer and cook at 380degreesF for 15 minutes.
3. Divide everything between plates and serve right away.

NUTRITION: Calories: 220 Fat: 12g Fiber: 4g Carbs: 6g Protein: 9g

76. Crumbed Cod

Preparation Time: 15 minutes
Cooking Time: 7 minutes
Servings: 4
INGREDIENTS:

- 1 cup flour
- 4: 4ounce skinless codfish fillets, cut into rectangular pieces
- 6 eggs
- 2 green chilies, finely chopped
- 6 scallions, finely chopped
- 4 garlic cloves, minced
- Salt and black pepper, to taste
- 2 teaspoons soy sauce

DIRECTIONS:
1. Prepare the Air fryer to 375 degrees F and grease an Air fryer basket.
2. Place the flour in a shallow dish and mix remaining ingredients except cod in another shallow dish.
3. Coat each cod fillet into the flour and then dip in the egg mixture.
4. Arrange the cod fillets in the Air fryer basket and cook for about 7 minutes.
5. Dish out and serve warm.

NUTRITION: Calories: 462 Fat: 16.9g Carbohydrates: 51.3g Protein: 24.4g

77. Spicy Cod

Preparation Time: 5 minutes
Cooking Time: 10 minutes
Servings: 4
INGREDIENTS:
- 4 cod fillets; boneless
- 2 tbsp. assorted chili peppers
- 1 lemon; sliced
- Juice of 1 lemon
- Salt and black pepper to taste

DIRECTIONS:
1. In your air fryer, mix the cod with the chili pepper, lemon juice, salt, and pepper
2. Arrange the lemon slices on top and cook at 360degreesF for 10 minutes.
3. Divide the fillets between plates and serve.

NUTRITION: Calories: 102 Fat: 8g Carbs: 1g Protein: 8g

78. Haddock with Cheese Sauce

Preparation Time: 15 minutes
Cooking Time: 8 minutes

Servings: 4
INGREDIENTS:
- 4: 6ounce haddock fillets
- 6 tablespoons fresh basil, chopped
- 4 tablespoons pine nuts
- 2 tablespoons Parmesan cheese, grated
- 2 tablespoons olive oil
- Salt and black pepper, to taste

DIRECTIONS:
1. Ready the Air fryer to 360 degrees F and grease an Air fryer basket.
2. Season the haddock fillets with salt and black pepper and coat evenly with olive oil.
3. Transfer the haddock fillets to the Air fryer basket and cook for about 8 minutes.
4. Put the remaining ingredients in a food processor and pulse until smooth to make cheese sauce.
5. Dish out the haddock fillets in the bowl and top with cheese sauce to serve.

NUTRITION: Calories: 354 Fat: 17.5g Carbohydrates: 1.7g Protein: 47g

79. Swordfish Steaks and Tomatoes

Preparation Time: 10 minutes
Cooking Time: 10 minutes
Servings: 2
INGREDIENTS:
- 30 oz. canned tomatoes; chopped.
- 2 1inch thick swordfish steaks
- 2 tbsp. capers, drained
- 1 tbsp. red vinegar
- 2 tbsp. Oregano; chopped.
- A pinch of salt and black pepper

DIRECTIONS:
1. 1.In pan that fits the air fryer, combine all the ingredients
2. Toss, put the pan in the fryer and cook at 390degreesF for 10 minutes, flipping the fish halfway
3. Divide the mix between plates and serve

NUTRITION: Calories: 280 Fat: 12g Carbs: 6g Protein: 11g

80. Roasted Red Snapper

Preparation Time: 5 minutes
Cooking Time: 15 minutes
Servings: 4
INGREDIENTS:

- 4 red snapper fillets; boneless
- 2 garlic cloves; minced
- 1 tbsp. hot chili paste
- 2 tbsp. olive oil
- 2 tbsp. coconut aminos
- 2 tbsp. lime juice
- A pinch of salt and black pepper

DIRECTIONS:

1. Take bowl and mix all the ingredients except the fish and whisk well
2. Rub the fish with this mix, place it in your air fryer's basket and cook at 380degreesF for 15 minutes
3. Serve with side salad.

NUTRITION: Calories: 220 Fat: 13g Carbs: 6g Protein: 11g

81. Lemony Flounder Fillets

Preparation Time: 5 minutes
Cooking Time: 12 minutes
Servings: 2
INGREDIENTS:

- 2 flounder fillets; boneless
- 2 garlic cloves; minced
- 2 tbsp. olive oil
- 2 tbsp. lemon juice
- 2 tsp. coconut aminos
- 1/2 tsp. stevia

- A pinch of salt and black pepper

DIRECTIONS:

1. In pan that fits your air fryer mix all the ingredients.
2. Toss, and cook at 390 degrees F for 12 minutes.
3. Divide into bowls and serve.

NUTRITION: Calories: 251 Fat: 13g Carbs: 5g Protein: 10g

82. Sea Bass Paella

Preparation Time: 10 minutes
Cooking Time: 25 minutes
Servings: 4
INGREDIENTS:

- 1 lb. sea bass fillets; cubed
- 1 red bell pepper; deseeded and chopped.
- 6 scallops
- 8 shrimp; peeled and deveined
- 5 oz. wild rice
- 2 oz. peas
- 14 oz. dry white wine
- 3 1/2 oz. chicken stock
- A drizzle of olive oil
- Salt and black pepper to taste

DIRECTIONS:

1. In heatproof dish that fits your air fryer, place all the ingredients and toss.
2. Place the dish in your air fryer and cook at 380degreesF for 25 minutes, stirring halfway.
3. Divide between plates and serve.

NUTRITION: Calories: 710 Fat: 37g Carbs: 68g Protein: 51g

DIABETICS AIR FRYER POULTRY

83. Low Fat Butter Chicken

Preparation Time: 10 minutes
Cooking Time: 20 minutes
Servings: 4
INGREDIENTS:

- Salt
- Fresh coriander
- 6 large red tomatoes
- 400g of chicken chunks, sliced
- 4 large onions
- 4 Green chilies (should be slit from the middle and deseeded)
- 4 Cloves
- 3 Cinnamon sticks
- 2 bay leaves
- 2 teaspoons of oil
- 2 Cardamom
- 1/4 teaspoon of turmeric
- 1/4 cup of yogurt/curd
- 1/2 teaspoon of red chili
- 1/2 teaspoon of coriander powder
- 1 tablespoon of garlic pastes

DIRECTIONS:

1. Cut onion into slices and add the slices to garlic paste, cardamom, Bay Leaves, and cinnamon.
2. Sauté the mixture until the onion slices get browned.
3. Add yogurt and chopped tomatoes to the mixture and blend into a paste.
4. Sauté the chicken in the left-over oil of onions.
5. When the chicken is almost done, add onion and tomato paste to it.
6. Now, you can add green chilies, turmeric, coriander powder, salt, and red chili to the chicken.
7. Continue cooking the chicken until its oil begins to float on top.
8. You can now garnish it before you serve it.

NUTRITION: Calories: 150 Fat: 7g Carbohydrates: 33g Protein: 12g

84. Chicken Kebabs with Pistachio Gremolata

Preparation Time:
Cooking Time:
Servings:
INGREDIENTS:

- For Chicken Kebabs:
- 1/4cup of olive oil
- 1/4cup of fresh lemon juice
- 1/4teaspoon of freshly ground black pepper
- 1/2cup of Greek yogurt
- 1/2teaspoon of garlic powder
- 1/2teaspoon of onion powder
- 3 pounds of boneless skinless chicken breasts or thighs, cut into 1 1/2" cubes
- 1 tablespoon of honey
- 2 teaspoons of sea salt
- 1 teaspoon of culinary grade lavender buds
- For Pistachio Gremolata:
- 3/4 cup of olive oil
- 1/4 teaspoon of freshly ground black pepper to taste
- 1/2 cup of Wonderful Pistachios No Shells finely chopped
- 2 teaspoons of culinary grade lavender buds optional
- 1/2 teaspoon of sea salt to taste
- 1 cup of flat-leaf parsley finely chopped
- Zest of 2 medium lemons finely grated
- 2 garlic cloves finely minced

DIRECTIONS:

1. Combine yogurt, olive oil, lemon juice, and the remaining marinade ingredients. Whisk well to combine. Pour over chicken.
2. Toss to make chicken coated. You can refrigerate it overnight or for at least, 1 hour.
3. For gremolata, add pepper, salt, lavender, garlic, lemon zest, pistachios, and parsley together.

4. 3.Add half cup of olive oil to it before you stir it very well. You should also cover and refrigerate it until when you want to serve it.
5. Air fry the kebabs for 4 minutes. Turn them over and air fry them for another 3 minutes.
6. Reduce the heat and cook it for another 5 minutes. This will allow the chicken to be thoroughly cooked without burning on the outside.
7. Serve the chicken kebabs with some gremolata and sauce.

NUTRITION: Calories: 121 Fat: 4g Carbohydrates: 23g Protein: 7g

85. Hawaiian Chicken Packet

Preparation Time: 15 minutes
Cooking Time: 20 minutes
Servings: 4
INGREDIENTS:

- 4 skinless, boneless chicken breast halves
- 1 red bell pepper, seeded and sliced into strips
- 1 onion, chopped
- 1 green bell pepper
- 1 cup of bottled teriyaki sauce or marinade
- 1 can of pineapple chunks, drained

DIRECTIONS:
1. Preheat your air fryer to medium-high heat
2. Seeded and sliced bell pepper into strips
3. Spread aluminum foil on your countertop and place a piece of chicken in the center.
4. Coat the chicken with the teriyaki sauce by pouring the sauce on the chicken.
5. Sprinkle some pineapple chunks, onions, red peppers, and green peppers on the piece of chicken.
6. Fold the foil and seal it. Do the same to other pieces of chicken.
7. Cook them in your air fryer for 20 minutes. You may need to take one piece out to check its doneness before removing the other pieces of chicken.
8. You can now serve them.

NUTRITION: Calories: 304.1 Fat: 1.7g Protein: 33g Carbohydrates: 38.9g

86. Turkey and Zucchini Burgers with Corn on the Cob

Preparation Time: 15 minutes
Cooking Time: 15 – 20 minutes
Servings: 4
INGREDIENTS:

- 5 ounces of ground turkey breast
- 4 1/4-inch-thick slices of pepper Jack cheese (1 oz.)
- 3 tablespoons of panko breadcrumbs
- 3 tablespoons of finely chopped red or yellow onion
- 2 whole-wheat hamburger rolls, split and toasted
- 2 teaspoons of mayonnaise
- 2 teaspoons of low-fat plain yogurt
- 2 tablespoons of finely chopped jalapeño pepper
- 1 1/4 cups of thinly sliced red cabbage
- 1 tablespoon of lime juice
- 1 tablespoon and 1/2 teaspoon of canola oil
- 1 ear corn, husked and halved
- 3/4 teaspoon of chili powder
- 1/2 teaspoon of ground cumin
- 1/2 cup of shredded zucchini
- 1/4 teaspoon of salt
- 1/8 teaspoon of ground pepper

DIRECTIONS:
1. Add 1/8 teaspoon of salt, 1 tablespoon of oil, lime juice, jalapeno, and cabbage together in a bowl. In another bowl, you should combine the chili powder with the yogurt and mayonnaise.
2. Brush the corn with 1/2 teaspoon of oil.
3. Add 1/8 teaspoon of salt with pepper, cumin, onion, panko, zucchini, and turkey. Marsh and the items together into a paste-like mixture.
4. Cook the corn for about 7 to 10 minutes. Also, you should heat the patties until they are browned. This should take about 5 minutes of continuous heating.

5. Top the patties with cheese slices before they are done. This will allow the cheese to melt.

6. Put mayonnaise mixture on the cut sides of the hamburger rolls.

7. Divide the remaining slaw on the rolls. Top the burger with the roll tops and the patties before cutting the corn into half.

8. Serve half corn with a whole burger.

NUTRITION: Calories: 446 Fat: 19g Carbohydrates: 43g Protein: 21g

87. Long-Roasted Chicken Thighs

Preparation Time: 10 minutes
Cooking Time: 3 hours
Servings: 4
INGREDIENTS:
- Kosher salt
- 8 skin-on, bone-in chicken thighs
- 4 cloves of garlic (should be sliced)
- 4 bay leaves, torn in half
- Black pepper

DIRECTIONS:
1. Season the chicken a day or two before you cook this recipe.
2. Sprinkle some salt on both sides of the chicken thighs.
3. Mix the garlic, bay leaves, and black pepper together. Coat the chicken thighs in the mixture before you refrigerate them for at least 24 hours.
4. Preheat your air fryer and cook the chicken thighs at 350 degrees F for up to 2 hours.
5. Reduce the heat to 325 degrees F and cook it for another 1 hour. This will make the chicken thighs crispy, but they will also shrink in size. They will be golden brown.
6. You can now serve them with vegetable salad.

NUTRITION: Calories: 225 Fat: 14g Carbohydrates: 3g Protein: 20

88. Mini Turkey Meatballs

Preparation Time: 15 minutes
Cooking Time: 10 minutes
Servings: 5

INGREDIENTS:
- 3 tablespoons of olive oil
- 3 tablespoons of ketchup
- 3 garlic cloves, minced
- 1/4 teaspoon of ground black pepper
- 1/4 cup of grated Pecorino Romano
- 1/4 cup of grated Parmesan
- 1/4 cup of dried breadcrumbs
- 1/4 cup of Italian parsley leaves, chopped
- 1 teaspoon of salt
- 1 small onion, grated
- 1 pound of ground dark turkey meat
- 1 large egg

DIRECTIONS:
1. Get a big bowl. Add pepper, salt, Pecorino, Parmesan, parsley, ketchup, breadcrumbs, egg, garlic, and onion together.
2. Whisk them until they mix evenly. Add the turkey and mix them.
3. Shape the mixture into several meatballs. Air fry the meatballs for about 5 minutes. They should be brown by them.
4. Now prepare your favorite sauce and dredge the meatballs in it.
5. You can now serve the turkey meatballs. They are best served either warm or hot.

NUTRITION: Calories: 48 Fat: 10g Carbohydrates: 3g Protein: 3g

89. White Chicken Chili

Preparation Time: 10 minutes
Cooking Time: 45 minutes
Servings: 4
INGREDIENTS:
- 1 pound of boneless skinless chicken breasts (should be chopped)
- 1 medium onion (to be chopped)
- 1 tablespoon of olive oil
- 2 garlic cloves, minced
- 2 cans of chicken broth
- 1 can of chopped green chiles

DIRECTIONS:
1. Cook both chicken and onion in oil until they are browned. Add the garlic before you cook the mixture a minute more.
2. Stir in cayenne, oregano, cumin, chiles, and the broth and boil them together.

3. Mash a can of beans until it becomes like a paste. Add it to a saucepan and add the remaining beans to the same saucepan.
4. Add the chicken to the beans and cook them at low heat for about 30 minutes or until the chicken changes its color from pink and the onion is tender.
5. You can now serve it with cheese and jalapeno pepper.

NUTRITION: Calories: 219 Fat: 7g Carbohydrates: 21g Protein: 19g

90. Herbed Chicken Marsala

Preparation Time: 10 minutes
Cooking Time: 30 minutes
Servings: 4
INGREDIENTS:
- Kosher salt and freshly ground black pepper
- 4-ounce boneless, skinless chicken breast cutlets
- 3/4 cup of low-sodium chicken broth
- 2 teaspoons of unsalted butter
- 2 tablespoons fresh flat-leaf parsley, roughly chopped
- 10 ounces of white button or cremini (baby Bella) mushrooms, sliced
- 1/3 cup of whole wheat flour
- 1/3 cup of sweet marsala wine
- 1/3 cup of sun-dried tomatoes (not packed in oil; not rehydrated), finely chopped or very thinly sliced
- 1/2 teaspoon of chopped fresh rosemary
- 1 1/2 tablespoon of extra-virgin olive oil

DIRECTIONS:
1. Pound the chicken cutlets to flatten it. Sprinkle it with 1/4 teaspoon each of salt and pepper.
2. Coat the chicken with flour and air fry it for about 4 minutes. It should be golden brown by then. Place it in an airtight container to keep it warm.
3. After removing the chicken, add rosemary, sun-dried tomatoes, and 1/2 cup of the chicken broth to what is left in the fryer after the chicken is removed. Cook the mixture for a minute.

4. Mix the mushrooms with 1/2 teaspoon of pepper and 1/4 teaspoon of salt. Cook the mixture for 5 minutes to make the mushrooms soft.
5. Add marsala to the mushroom mixture and boil them together.
6. Add the remaining 1/4 cup of broth to the butter and cook them with low heat to melt the butter. This should not exceed 30 seconds.
7. Top the chicken with the sauce and mushroom mixture before you serve it. You should also sprinkle it with some parsley.

NUTRITION: Calories: 294 Fat: 11g Protein: 30g Carbohydrates: 19g

91. Chicken Alfredo

Preparation Time: 10 minutes
Cooking Time: 25 – 30 minutes
Servings: 4
INGREDIENTS:
- Some Kosher salt
- Freshly ground black pepper
- Freshly chopped parsley, for garnish
- 8 oz. of fettuccini
- 2 tablespoons of extra-virgin olive oil
- 2 cloves garlic, minced
- 2 boneless skinless chicken breasts
- 1/2 cup of heavy cream
- 1 cup of freshly grated Parmesan
- 1 1/2 cup of whole milk
- 1 1/2 cup of low-sodium chicken broth

DIRECTIONS:
1. The first thing to do is to heat the olive oil.
2. Add the chicken, a pinch of salt, and pepper to the oil and cook it in your air fryer.
3. Cook it for about 8 minutes, which will make it turn crispy and golden.
4. Get the chicken and let it cool for 10 minutes before you slice it.
5. Mix the garlic with the milk and broth. Add pepper and salt to the mixture.
6. Stir fettuccine into the mixture. Cook it until it becomes thick and firm. This should not exceed 8 minutes.

7. Stir the parmesan and cream into the broth mixture. Leave it for some time to allow it to thicken.
8. Remove the broth from the air fryer and add your slices of chicken into it. Now, you can garnish it with parsley. That's all. You can now serve it.

NUTRITION: Calories: 310 Fat: 17g Carbohydrates: 23g Protein: 17g

92. Turkey Breast

Preparation Time: 20 minutes
Cooking Time: 35 minutes
Servings:
INGREDIENTS:
- 4 pound of turkey breast, with the rib removed
- 2 teaspoons of kosher salt
- 1/2 tablespoon of dry turkey or poultry seasoning
- 1 tablespoon of olive oil

DIRECTIONS:
1. Coat the turkey breast with 1/2 tablespoon of oil.
2. The next step is to season both sides of the turkey breast with salt and turkey seasoning. You can add the remaining oil to the seasoned turkey.
3. Preheat your air fryer to 350 degrees F before cooking the turkey for 20 minutes.
4. Turn it over and cook it at 160 degrees F for another 30 to 35 minutes.
5. Let it cool for 10 minutes before you carve it.

NUTRITION: Calories: 226 Protein: 32.5g Fat: 10g Carbs: 0.3g

93. Turkey and Cream Cheese Breast Pillows

Preparation Time: 5 minutes
Cooking time: 10 minutes
Servings: 4
INGREDIENTS:
- 1 cup of milk with 1 egg inside (put the egg in the cup and then fill with milk)
- 1/3 cup of water
- 1/4 cup olive oil or oil

- 1 and 3/4 teaspoon of salt
- 2 tbsp sugar
- 2 and 1/2 tbsp dried granular yeast
- 4 cups of flour
- 1 egg yolk to brush
- 2 jars of cream cheese
- 15 slices of turkey breast cut in 4

DIRECTION:
1. Mix all the dough ingredients with your hands until it is very smooth. After the ready dough, make small balls and place on a floured surface. Reserve
2. Open each dough ball with a roller trying to make it square. Cut squares of approximately 10 X 10 cm. Fill with a piece of turkey breast and 1 teaspoon of
3. cream cheese coffee. Close the union of the masses joining the 4 points. Brush with the egg yolk and set aside.
4. Preheat the air fryer. Set the timer of 5 minutes and the temperature to 200C.
5. Place 6 units in the air fryer's basket and bake for 4 or 5 minutes at 180C.
6. Repeat until all the pillows have finished cooking.

NUTRITION: Calories: 538 Fat: 29.97g Carbohydrates: 22.69g Protein: 43.64g

94. Chicken Wings

Preparation Time: 10 minutes
Cooking time: 25 minutes
Servings: 2
INGREDIENTS:
- 10 chicken wings (about 700g)
- Oil in spay
- 1 tbsp soy sauce
- 1/2 tbsp cornstarch
- 2 tbsp honey
- 1 tbsp ground fresh chili paste
- 1 tbsp minced garlic
- 1/2 tsp chopped fresh ginger
- 1 tbsp lime sumo
- 1/2 tbsp salt
- 2 tbsp chives

DIRECTION:
1. Dry the chicken with a tea towel. Cover the chicken with the oil spray.

2. Place the chicken inside the hot air electric fryer, separating the wings towards the edge to not be on top of each other.
3. Cook at 200C until the skin is crispy for about 25 min. Turn them around half the time.
4. Mix the soy sauce with cornstarch in a small pan. Add honey, chili paste, garlic, ginger, and lime sumo.
5. Simmer until it boils and thickens.
6. Put chicken in a bowl, add the sauce and cover all the chicken. Sprinkle with chives.

NUTRITION: Calories: 81 Fat: 5.4g Carbohydrates: 0g Protein: 7.46g

95. Pickled Poultry

Preparation Time: 10 minutes
Cooking time: 25 minutes
Servings: 4
INGREDIENTS:

- 600g of poultry, without bones or skin
- 3 white onions, peeled and cut into thin slices
- 5 garlic cloves, peeled and sliced
- 3 dl olive oil
- 1 dl apple cider vinegar
- 1/2 l white wine
- 2 bay leaves
- 5 g peppercorns
- Flour
- Pepper
- Salt

DIRECTION:
1. Rub the bird in dice that we will pepper and flour
2. Put oil in the prepared pan and heat. When the oil is hot, fry the floured meat dice in it until golden brown.
3. Take them out and reserve, placing them in a clay or oven dish. Strain the oil in which you have fried the meat
4. Preheat the oven to 170° C
5. Put the already cast oil in another pan over the fire. Sauté the garlic and onions in it. Add the white wine and let cook about 3 minutes.
6. Remove the pan from the heat, add the vinegar to the oil and wine. Remove,

rectify salt, and pour this mixture into the source where you had left the bird dice.
7. Put in the oven, lower the temperature to 140°C and bake for 1 and 1/2 hours. Remove the source from the oven and let it stand at room temperature
8. When the source is cold, put it in the fridge and let it rest a few hours before serving.

NUTRITION: Calories: 232 Fat: 15g Carbohydrates: 5.89g Protein: 18.2g

96. Rolls Stuffed with Broccoli and Carrots with Chicken

Preparation Time: 15 minutes
Cooking time: 25 minutes
Servings: 4
INGREDIENTS:

- 8 sheets of rice pasta
- 1 chicken breast
- 1 onion
- 1 carrot
- 150g broccolis
- 1 can of sweet corn
- Extra virgin olive oil
- Salt
- Ground pepper
- Soy sauce
- 1 bag of rice three delicacies

DIRECTION:
1. Start with the vegetable that you have to cook previously, stop them, peel the carrot.
2. Cut the carrot and broccoli as small as you can. Add the broccolis and the carrot to a pot with boiling water and cook a few minutes, they have to be tender, but not too much, that crunch a little.
3. Drain well and reserve. Cut the onion into julienne. Cut the breast into strips.
4. In the Wok, put some extra virgin olive oil.
5. Add to the wok when it is hot, the onion and the chicken breast. Sauté well until the chicken is cooked.
6. Drain the corn and add to the wok along with the broccolis and the carrot.

7. Sauté so that the ingredients are mixed. Add salt, ground pepper and a little soy sauce.
8. Mix well and let the filling cool. Hydrate the rice pasta sheets.
9. Spread on the worktable and distribute the filling between the sheets of rice paste.
10. Assemble the rolls and paint with a little oil.
11. Put in the air fryer, those who enter do not pile up. Select 10 minutes 200 degrees C.
12. Select 180 degrees C, 5 minutes.
13. Make while the rice as indicated by the manufacturer in its bag.
14. Serve the rice with the rolls.

NUTRITION: Calories: 125 Fat: 4.58g Carbohydrates: 16.83g Protein: 4.69g

97. Spicy Chicken Strips

Preparation Time: 5 minutes
Cooking time: 12 minutes
Servings: 5
INGREDIENTS:
- 1 cup buttermilk
- 1 1/2 tbsp hot pepper sauce
- 1 tsp salt
- 1/2 tsp black pepper, divided
- 1 pound boneless and skinless chicken breasts
- 3/4 cup panko breadcrumbs
- 1/2 tsp salt
- 1/4 tsp hot pepper, or to taste
- 1 tbsp olive oil

DIRECTION:
1. Cut the boneless chicken breast into 3/4-inch strips
2. Put the buttermilk, hot sauce, salt and 1/4 teaspoon of black pepper in shallow bowl.
3. Put the chicken strips and refrigerate for at least two hours. Put breadcrumbs, salt, and the remaining black pepper and hot pepper in another bowl; Add and stir the oil.
4. Get the chicken strips from the marinade and discard the marinade.
5. Put the strips, few at the same time, to the crumb mixture. Press the crumbs to the strips to achieve a uniform and firm cover.

6. Put half of the strips in single layer inside the basket. Cook at 350F for 12 minutes. Cook the rest when the first batch is cooked.

NUTRITION: Calories: 207 Fat: 9g Carbohydrates: 5g Protein: 25g

98. Chicken In Wheat Cake With Aioli Sauce

Preparation Time: 10 minutes
Cooking time: 35 minutes
Servings: 4
INGREDIENTS:
- 500g breaded chicken
- 4 wheat cakes
- Extra virgin olive oil
- 1 small lettuce
- Grated cheese
- Aioli sauce

DIRECTION:
1. Put the breaded chicken in the air fryer with a little extra virgin olive oil and fry at 180 degrees for 20 minutes.
2. Take out and reserve.
3. Chop the lettuce. Put the wheat cakes on the worktable and distribute the chopped lettuce between them.
4. On the chopped lettuce spread the pieces of breaded chicken.
5. Cover with grated cheese and add some aioli sauce.
6. Close the wheat cakes and place on the baking sheet.
7. Take to the oven, 180 degrees, 15 minutes or until the cheese is melted.

NUTRITION: Calories: 91 Fat: 9.83g Carbohydrates: 1.06g Protein: 0.19g

99. Soy Chicken and Sesame

Preparation Time: 10 minutes
Cooking time: 50 minutes
Servings: 4
INGREDIENTS:
- 1 large chicken breast
- 2 Eggs
- 1/2 cup Breadcrumbs
- 1/2 tsp. Extra virgin olive oil

- 1/4 tbsp. Salt
- Ground pepper, to taste
- 1/2 cup Soy sauce
- 1/4 cup Sesame

DIRECTION:
1. Cut the breast into fillets and put in a bowl.
2. Season the chicken.
3. Add soy sauce and sesame. Mix well and leave 30 minutes.
4. Beat the eggs. Cover all the steaks through the beaten egg and the breadcrumbs.
5. With a silicone brush, permeate the fillets well on both sides.
6. Place on the grill of the air fryer and select 180 degrees C, 20 minutes.
7. Make the fillets in batches so that they pile against each other.

NUTRITION: Calories: 373 Fat: 18.30g Carbohydrates: 6.24g Proteins: 34.74g

100. Chicken with Provencal Herbs and Potatoes

Preparation Time: 10 minutes
Cooking time: 55 minutes
Servings: 2
INGREDIENTS:
- 4 potatoes
- 2 chicken hindquarters
- Provencal herbs
- Salt to taste
- 1/4 tsp. Ground pepper, or to taste
- 1/2 tsp. Extra virgin olive oil

DIRECTION:
1. Peel the potatoes and cut into slices.
2. Pepper and put on the grid of the base air fryer.
3. Impregnate the chicken well with oil, salt and pepper and put some Provencal herbs.
4. Place the chicken on the potatoes.
5. Take the grill to the bucket of the air fryer and put inside.
6. Select 170 degrees C and cook 40 minutes.
7. Turn the chicken and leave 15 more minutes.

NUTRITION: Calories: 198.5 Fat: 4.2g Carbohydrates: 17.6g Protein: 21.7g

101. Salted Biscuit Pie Turkey Chops

Preparation Time: 5 minutes
Cooking time: 20 minutes
Servings: 4
INGREDIENTS:
- 8 large turkey chops
- 300 gr of crackers
- 2 eggs
- 1/2 tsp. Extra virgin olive oil
- Salt to taste
- Ground pepper to taste

DIRECTION:
1. Put the turkey chops on the worktable, and salt and pepper.
2. Beat the eggs in a bowl.
3. Crush the cookies in the Thermomix with a few turbo strokes until they are made grit, or you can crush them with the blender.
4. Put the cookies in a bowl.
5. Pass the chops through the beaten egg and then passed them through the crushed cookies. Press well so that the empanada is perfect.
6. Paint the empanada with a silicone brush and extra virgin olive oil.
7. Put the chops in the basket of the air fryer, not all will enter. They will be done in batches.
8. Select 200 degrees C, 15 minutes.
9. When you have all the chops made, serve.

NUTRITION: Calories: 126 Fat: 6g Carbohydrates 0g Protein: 18g

102. Baked Tomato Chicken

Preparation Time: 10 minutes
Cooking Time: 20 minutes
Servings: 2
INGREDIENTS:
- 3 tablespoons olive oil
- 1/2-pint grape tomatoes
- 6 pitted Greek olives, sliced
- 2 boneless skinless chicken breast halves
- 1/4 teaspoon salt
- 1/4 teaspoon pepper
- 2 tablespoons capers, drained

DIRECTIONS:

1. Flavor chicken with ground black pepper and salt.
2. Place Instant Pot over kitchen platform. Place Air Fryer Lid on top. Press Air Fry set the temperature to 375°F and set the timer to 5 minutes to preheat. Press Start and allow it to preheat for 5 minutes.
3. Take Air Fryer Basket, grease it with some cooking spray. In the basket, add the chicken. Add the remaining ingredients and stir.

4. Place the basket in the inner pot of Instant Pot, close Air Fryer Lid on top.
5. Press the "Bake" setting. Set temperature to 330°F and set the timer to 15 minutes. Press Start.
6. Open Air Fryer Lid after cooking time is over. Serve warm.

NUTRITION: Calories: 331 Fat: 17g Carbohydrates: 7g Protein: 35g

DIABETICS AIR FRYER MEAT

103. Roast Beef

Preparation Time: 5minutes
Cooking Time: 45 minutes
Servings: 3
INGREDIENTS:

- 3-1/2 lbs. beef roast
- 2 tbsps. olive oil
- 1 tbsp. rosemary
- 1/2 tbsp. garlic powder
- 1/2 tsp fresh ground rugged black pepper

DIRECTIONS:

1. Change temperature of the air fryer to 360°F
2. Mix herbs and oil on a plate. Roll the roast in the blend on the plate to ensure that the beef's entire surface is covered.
3. Set the beef in the air fryer basket. Establish the timer for 45 mins for tool-rare beef, 51 mins for the tool. Examine the beef with a meat thermostat to see if it is done to your liking.
4. Cook for extra 6-minute periods if you like it cooked a lot more. Keep in mind that the roast will undoubtedly remain to prepare while it is relaxing.
5. Eliminate the roast from the air fryer and put on a plate, cover with lightweight aluminum foil. Allow it to rest for 10 minutes before serving.

NUTRITION: Calories: 666 Carbs: 0.3g Fat: 54g Proteins: 43g

104. Bacon

Preparation Time: 5 minutes
Cooking Time: 10 minutes
Servings: 4
INGREDIENTS:

- 11 slices bacon

DIRECTIONS:

1. Cut bacon in half and place the first half in the air fryer.
2. Set the temperature at 401 degrees F and set the timer to 11 minutes.

3. Check it halfway through to see if anything needs to be rearranged.
4. Cook remainder of the time. Serve.

NUTRITION: Calories: 91 Carbs: 0.2g Protein: 2g Fat: 5g

105. Beef Empanadas

Preparation Time: 10 minutes
Cooking Time: 20 minutes
Servings: 3
INGREDIENTS:

- 8 Goya empanada discs, defrosted
- 1 cup picadillo
- 1 egg white, blended
- 1 tsp. water
- Cooking spray

DIRECTIONS:

1. Set air fryer at 325 degrees F.
2. Apply a cooking spray to the basket.
3. Place 2 tbsps. of picadillo to each disc space. Fold in half and secure using a fork. Do the same for all the dough.
4. Mix water and egg whites. Sprinkle to empanadas top.
5. Set 3 of them in your air fryer and allow to bake for minutes. Set aside and do the same for the remaining empanadas.

Nutrition: Calories: 183 Carbs: 22g Protein: 11 g Fat: 5g

106. Pork Rind

Preparation Time: 10 minutes
Cooking Time: 1 hour
Servings: 4
INGREDIENTS:

- 1kg pork rinds
- Salt to taste
- 1/2 tsp black pepper coffee

DIRECTION:

1. Preheat the air fryer. Set the time of 5 minutes and the temperature to 2000C.
2. Cut the bacon into cubes - 1 finger wide.
3. Flavor with salt and a pinch of pepper.

4. Put the basket of the air fryer. Set the time of 45 minutes and press the power button.
5. Shake the basket every 10 minutes so that the pork rinds stay golden brown equally.
6. Once they are ready, drain a little on the paper towel, so they stay dry.
7. Transfer to a plate and serve.

NUTRITION: Calories: 83 Fat: 7 Carbs: 0g Protein: 4g

107. Pork Fillets with Serrano Ham

Preparation Time: 10 minutes
Cooking Time: 20 minutes
Servings: 4
INGREDIENTS:
- 400g of very thin sliced pork fillets
- 2 boiled and chopped eggs
- 100g chopped Serrano ham
- 1 beaten egg
- Breadcrumbs

DIRECTION:
1. Make a roll with the pork fillets. Introduce half-cooked egg and Serrano ham. So that the roll does not lose its shape, fasten with a string or chopsticks.
2. Pass the rolls through the beaten egg and then through the breadcrumbs until it forms a good layer.
3. Adjust the temperature of the air fryer for a few minutes at 180° C.
4. Insert the rolls in the basket and set the timer for about 8 minutes at 180º C.
5. Serve.

NUTRITION: Calories: 424 Fat: 15.15g Carbs: 37.47g Protein: 31.84g

108. Pork on A Blanket

Preparation Time: 5 minutes
Cooking Time: 10 minutes
Servings: 4
INGREDIENTS:
- 1/2 puff defrosted pastry sheet
- 16 thick smoked sausages
- 15 ml of milk

DIRECTION:

1. Prepare air fryer and set to 200°C. Timer to 5 minutes.
2. Cut the puff pastry into 64 x 38 mm strips.
3. Place a cocktail sausage at the end of the puff pastry and roll around the sausage, sealing the dough with some water.
4. Brush the top of the sausages wrapped in milk and place them in the preheated air fryer.
5. Cook for 10 minutes at 200 degrees C until golden brown.

NUTRITION: Calories: 242 Fat: 14g Carbs: 0g Protein: 27g

109. Provencal Ribs

Preparation Time: 10 minutes
Cooking Time: 1 hour and 20 minutes
Servings: 4
INGREDIENTS:
- 500g of pork ribs
- Provencal herbs
- Salt
- Ground pepper
- 1/2 tsp. Oil

DIRECTION:
1. Prepare the ribs in a bowl and add some oil, Provencal herbs, salt, and ground pepper.
2. Stir well and leave in the fridge for at least 1 hour.
3. Put the ribs in the basket of the air fryer and select 200 C for 20 minutes.
4. From time to time, shake the basket and remove the ribs.

NUTRITION: Calories: 296 Fat: 22.63g Carbs: 0g Protein: 21.71g

110. Marinated Loin Potatoes

Preparation Time: 30 minutes
Cooking Time: 1 hour
Servings: 2
INGREDIENTS:
- 2 medium potatoes
- 4 fillets of marinated loin
- A little extra virgin olive oil
- Salt to taste

DIRECTION:

1. Peel the potatoes and cut. Cut with match-sized mandolin, potatoes with a cane but very thin.
2. Wash and immerse in water 30 minutes. Drain and dry well.
3. Add a little oil and stir so that the oil permeates well in all the potatoes.
4. Go to the basket of the air fryer and distribute well.
5. Cook at 1600C for 10 minutes.
6. Take out the basket, shake so that the potatoes take off. Let the potato tender. If it is not, leave 5 more minutes.
7. Arrange the steaks on top of the potatoes.
8. Select 10 minutes, and 180 C for 5 minutes again.

NUTRITION: Calories: 136 Fat: 5.1g Carbs: 1.9g Protein: 20.7g

111. Pork Tenderloin

Preparation Time: 10 minutes
Cooking Time: 20 minutes
Servings: 6
INGREDIENTS:

- 1/2 lb. pork tenderloin patted dry
- Non-stick cooking spray
- 2 tbsps. garlic scape pesto
- Salt
- Pepper

DIRECTIONS:

1. Change the Air Fryer temperature to 375 degrees F.
2. Massage all sides of the tenderloin with the non-stick cooking spray
3. Add pepper, garlic scape pesto, and salt.
4. Sprinkle the Air Fryer basket with cooking spray.
5. Place the tenderloin on the Air Fryer.
6. Cook the meal at 400°F for 10 minutes.
7. Turn each side and cook for another 10 minutes on the first side.
8. Remove the food from the air fryer.
9. Serve

NUTRITION: Calories: 379 Protein: 8.4g Fat: 2.2g Carbs: 0g

112. Roast Pork

Preparation Time: 10 minutes
Cooking Time: 50 minutes
Servings: 6
Ingredients:

- 2 lbs. pork loin
- 1 Tbsp. olive oil
- 1 tsp. salt

DIRECTIONS:

1. Change temperature of the Air Fryer to 360 F.
2. Apply the oil on the pork.
3. Add salt.
4. Cook the pork in the Air Fryer for about 50 minutes. Shake the food halfway through the cooking
5. Remove the meal from Air Fryer and allow it to cool.
6. Serve

NUTRITION: Calories: 150 Fat: 6g Carbs: 0g Protein: 23.1g

113. Pork Bondiola Chop

Preparation Time: 5 minutes
Cooking Time: 20 minutes
Servings: 4
INGREDIENTS:

- 1kg bondiola in pieces
- Breadcrumbs
- 2 beaten eggs
- Seasoning to taste

DIRECTIONS:

1. Cut the bondiola into small pieces
2. Add seasonings to taste.
3. Pour the beaten eggs on the seasoned bondiola.
4. Add the breadcrumbs.
5. Cook in the air fryer for 20 minutes while turning the food halfway.
6. Serve

NUTRITION: Calories: 265 Fat: 20.36g Carbs: 0g Protein: 19.14g

114. Fried Pork Chops

Preparation Time: 5 minutes
Cooking Time: 35 minutes

Servings: 2
INGREDIENTS:
- 3 cloves ground garlic
- 2 tbsps. olive oil
- 1 tbsp. of marinade
- 4 thawed pork chops

DIRECTIONS:
1. In a bowl, mix the cloves of ground garlic, oil, and marinade.
2. Apply the mixture on the pork chops.
3. Put the chops in the air fryer and cook at 360 C for 35 minutes.

NUTRITION: Calories: 118 Fat: 6.85g Carbs: 0g Protein: 13.12g

115. Steak

Preparation Time: 5 minutes
Cooking Time: 15 minutes
Servings: 2
INGREDIENTS:
- 1 Ribeye Steak or New York City Strip Steak
- Salt and Pepper
- Garlic Powder
- Paprika
- Butter

DIRECTIONS:
1. Place the meat to sit in a bowl at room temperature level.
2. Spray the olive oil onto both sides of the steak.
3. Add salt and pepper to season.
4. Add the garlic powder and paprika to the mixture.
5. Adjust the temperature of the air fryer to 400F.
6. Put steak in the air fryer and cook for 12 minutes flipping it halfway through.
7. Lead it with butter when ready, then serve.

NUTRITION: Calories: 301 Fat: 23g Carbs: 0g Protein: 23g

116. Flavored Rib Eye Steak

Preparation Time: 10 minutes
Cooking Time: 20 minutes
Servings: 4
INGREDIENTS:

- 2 pounds rib eye steak
- Salt and black pepper to the taste
- 1 tablespoons olive oil
- For the rub:
- 3 tablespoons sweet paprika
- 2 tablespoons onion powder
- 2 tablespoons garlic powder
- 1 tablespoon brown sugar
- 2 tablespoons oregano, dried
- 1 tablespoon cumin, ground
- 1 tablespoon rosemary, dried

DIRECTIONS:
1. In a bowl, mix paprika with onion and garlic powder, sugar, oregano, rosemary, salt, pepper, and cumin, stir and rub steak with this mix.
2. Season steak with salt and pepper, rub again with the oil, position it in the air fryer and for 20 minutes boil at 400 degrees F, flipping them halfway.
3. Move the steak to a cutting board, slice and serve with a side salad.
4. Enjoy!

NUTRITION: Calories 320 Fat 8g Carbs 22g Protein 21g

117. Chinese Steak and Broccoli

Preparation Time: 45 minutes
Cooking Time: 12 minutes
Servings: 4
INGREDIENTS:
- 3/4-pound round steak, cut into strips
- 1-pound broccoli florets
- 1/3 cup oyster sauce
- 2 teaspoons sesame oil
- 1 teaspoon soy sauce
- 1 teaspoon sugar
- 1/3 cup sherry
- 1 tablespoon olive oil
- 1 garlic clove, minced

DIRECTIONS:
1. In a bowl, mix sesame oil with oyster sauce, soy sauce, sherry, and sugar, stir well.

2. Add beef, toss, and leave aside for 30 minutes.
3. Transfer beef to a pan that fits your air fryer, add broccoli, garlic, and oil, toss everything.
4. Cook at 380 degrees F for 12 minutes.
5. Divide among plates and serve.
6. Enjoy!

NUTRITION: Calories 330 Fat 12g Carbs 23g Protein 23g

118. Provencal Pork

Preparation Time: 10 minutes
Cooking Time: 15 minutes
Servings: 2
INGREDIENTS:
- 1 red onion, sliced
- 1 yellow bell pepper, cut into strips
- 1 green bell pepper, cut into strips
- Salt and black pepper to the taste
- 2 teaspoons Provencal herbs
- 1/2 tablespoon mustard
- 1 tablespoon olive oil
- 7 ounces pork tenderloin

DIRECTIONS:
1. Using a baking dish in the air fryer, mix yellow bell pepper with green bell pepper, onion, salt, pepper, Provencal herbs, and half of the oil and toss well.
2. Season pork with salt, pepper, mustard, and the rest of the oil, toss well and add to veggies.
3. Introduce everything in your air fryer, cook at 370 degrees F for 15 minutes.
4. Divide among plates and serve.
5. Enjoy!

NUTRITION: Calories 300 Fat 8g Carbs 21g Protein 23g

119. Beef S trips with Snow Peas and Mushrooms

Preparation Time: 10 minutes
Cooking Time: 22 minutes
Servings: 2
INGREDIENTS:
- 2 beef steaks, cut into strips
- Salt and black pepper to the taste

- 7 ounces snow peas
- 8 ounces white mushrooms, halved
- 1 yellow onion, cut into rings
- 2 tablespoons soy sauce
- 1 teaspoon olive oil

DIRECTIONS:
1. In a bowl, mix olive oil with soy sauce, whisk, add beef strips and toss.
2. In another bowl, mix snow peas, onion and mushrooms with salt, pepper, and the oil, toss well, put in a pan that fits your air fryer and cook at 350 degrees F for 16 minutes.
3. Add beef strips to the pan as well and cook at 400 degrees F for 6 minutes more.
4. Divide everything on plates and serve.
5. Enjoy!

NUTRITION: Calories 235 Fat 8g Carbs 22g Protein 24g

120. Garlic Lamb Chops

Preparation Time: 10 minutes
Cooking Time: 10 minutes
Servings: 4
INGREDIENTS:
- 3 tablespoons olive oil
- 8 lamb chops
- Salt and black pepper to the taste
- 4 garlic cloves, minced
- 1 tablespoon oregano, chopped
- 1 tablespoon coriander, chopped

DIRECTIONS:
1. In a bowl, mix oregano with salt, pepper, oil, garlic, and lamb chops and toss to coat.
2. Transfer lamb chops to your air fryer and cook at 400 degrees F for 10 minutes.
3. Divide lamb chops on plates and serve with a side salad.
4. Enjoy!

NUTRITION: Calories 231 Fat 7g Carbs 14g Protein 23g

121. Crispy Lamb

Preparation Time: 10 minutes
Cooking Time: 30 minutes
Servings: 4
INGREDIENTS:

- 1 tablespoon breadcrumbs
- 2 tablespoons macadamia nuts, toasted and crushed
- 1 tablespoon olive oil
- 1 garlic clove, minced
- 28 ounces rack of lamb
- Salt and black pepper to the taste
- 1 egg
- 1 tablespoon rosemary, chopped

DIRECTIONS:
1. In a bowl, mix oil with garlic and stir well.
2. Season lamb with salt, pepper, and brush with the oil.
3. In another bowl, mix nuts with breadcrumbs and rosemary.
4. Get a separate bowl and break egg. Whisk well.
5. Dip lamb in egg, then in macadamia mix, place them in your air fryer's basket, cook at 360 degrees F and cook for 25 minutes, increase heat to 400 degrees F and cook for 5 minutes more.
6. Divide among plates and serve right away.
7. Enjoy!

NUTRITION: Calories 230 Fat 2g Carbs 10g Protein 12g

122. Indian Pork

Preparation Time: 10 minutes
Cooking Time: 35 minutes
Servings: 4
INGREDIENTS:
- 1 teaspoon ginger powder
- 2 teaspoons chili paste
- 2 garlic cloves, minced
- 14 ounces pork chops, cubed
- 1 shallot, chopped
- 1 teaspoon coriander, ground
- 7 ounces coconut milk
- 2 tablespoons olive oil
- 3 ounces peanuts, ground
- 3 tablespoons soy sauce
- Salt and black pepper to the taste

DIRECTIONS:
1. In a bowl, mix 1 teaspoon of raw gill with chili paste, half garlic, half soy sauce and

half oil, whisk, add the meat and let sit for 10 minutes.
2. Transfer the meat to an air fryer basket and cook at 400 degrees F for 12 minutes.
3. In the meantime, heat the pot over medium high heat with the remaining oil, add the shallots, the remaining garlic, coriander, coconut milk, the remaining peanuts, the remaining chili paste, and the remaining soy sauce and stir for 5 minutes.
4. Divide the pork into plates, spread the coconut mix on top and serve.
5. Enjoy!

NUTRITION: Calories 423 Fat 11g Carbs 42g Protein 18g

123. Lamb and Creamy Brussels Sprouts

Preparation Time: 10 minutes
Cooking Time: 1 hour and 10 minutes
Servings: 4
INGREDIENTS:
- 2 pounds leg of lamb, scored
- 2 tablespoons olive oil
- 1 tablespoon rosemary, chopped
- 1 tablespoon lemon thyme, chopped
- 1 garlic clove, minced
- and 1/2-pounds Brussels sprouts, trimmed
- 1 tablespoon butter, melted
- 1/2 cup sour cream
- Salt and black pepper to the taste

DIRECTIONS:
1. Season leg of lamb with salt, pepper, thyme and rosemary, brush with oil, place in your air fryer's basket, cook at 300 degrees F for 1 hour, and transfer to a plate keep warm.
2. Using a pan for the air fryer, mix Brussels sprouts with salt, pepper, garlic, butter and sour cream, toss, put in your air fryer and cook at 400 degrees F for 10 minutes.
3. Divide lamb on plates, add Brussels sprouts on the side and serve.
4. Enjoy!

NUTRITION: Calories 440 Fat 23g Carbs 2g Protein 49g

124. Beef Fillets with Garlic Mayo

Preparation Time: 10 minutes
Cooking Time: 40 minutes
Servings: 8
INGREDIENTS:

- 1 cup mayonnaise
- 1/3 cup sour cream
- 2 garlic cloves, minced
- 3 pounds beef fillet
- 2 tablespoons chives, chopped
- 2 tablespoons mustard
- 2 tablespoons mustard
- 1/4 cup tarragon, chopped
- Salt and black pepper to the taste

DIRECTIONS:

1. Season beef with salt and pepper to the taste, place in your air fryer, cook at 370 degrees F for 20 minutes, transfer to a plate and leave aside for a few minutes.
2. In a bowl, mix garlic with sour cream, chives, mayo, salt and pepper, whisk and leave aside.
3. In another bowl, mix mustard with Dijon mustard and tarragon, whisk, add beef, toss, return to the air fryer and for 20 minutes boil at 350 degrees F .
4. Divide beef on plates, spread garlic mayo on top and serve.
5. Enjoy!

NUTRITION: Calories 235 Fat 11g Carbs 0.2g Protein 32g

125. Mustard Marinated Beef

Preparation Time: 10 minutes
Cooking Time: 45 minutes
Servings: 6
INGREDIENTS:

- 6 bacon strips
- 2 tablespoons butter
- 3 garlic cloves, minced
- Salt and black pepper to the taste
- 1 tablespoon horseradish
- 1 tablespoon mustard
- 3 pounds beef roast
- 1 and 3/4 cup beef stock

- 3/4 cup red wine

DIRECTIONS:

1. In a bowl, mix butter with mustard, garlic, salt, pepper and horseradish, whisk and rub beef with this mix.
2. Arrange bacon strips on a cutting board, place beef on top, fold bacon around beef, transfer to your air fryer's basket, cook at 400 degrees F for 15 minutes and transfer to a pan that fits your fryer.
3. Add stock and wine to beef, introduce pan in your air fryer and cook at 360 degrees F for 30 minutes more.
4. Carve beef, divide among plates, and serve with a side salad.
5. Enjoy!

NUTRITION: Calories 228 Fat 13g Carbs 3g Protein 23g

126. Marinated Pork Chops and Onions

Preparation Time: 24 hours
Cooking Time: 25 minutes
Servings: 6
INGREDIENTS:

- 2 pork chops
- 1/4 cup olive oil
- 2 yellow onions, sliced
- 2 garlic cloves, minced
- 2 teaspoons mustard
- 1 teaspoon sweet paprika
- Salt and black pepper to the taste
- 1/2 teaspoon oregano, dried
- 1/2 teaspoon thyme, dried
- A pinch of cayenne pepper

DIRECTIONS:

1. In a bowl, mix oil with garlic, mustard, paprika, black pepper, oregano, thyme, and cayenne and whisk well.
2. Combine onions with meat and mustard mix, toss to coat, cover, and keep in the fridge for 1 day.
3. Transfer meat and onions mix to a pan that fits your air fryer and cook at 360 degrees F for 25 minutes.
4. Divide everything on plates and serve.
5. Enjoy!

NUTRITION: Calories 384 Fat 4g Carbs 17g Protein 25g

127. Creamy Pork

Preparation Time: 10 minutes
Cooking Time: 22 minutes
Servings: 6
INGREDIENTS:

- 2 pounds pork meat, boneless and cubed
- 2 yellow onions, chopped
- 1 tablespoon olive oil
- 1 garlic clove, minced
- 3 cups chicken stock
- 2 tablespoons sweet paprika
- Salt and black pepper to the taste
- 2 tablespoons white flour

- 1 and 1/2 cups sour cream
- 2 tablespoons dill, chopped

DIRECTIONS:

1. Using a pan for the air fryer, mix pepper, salt and oil with the pork and rub well.
2. Put them all in the air fryer and for 7 minutes boil at 360 degrees F.
3. Add onion, garlic, stock, paprika, flour, sour cream, and dill, toss and cook at 370 degrees F for 15 minutes more.
4. Divide everything on plates and serve right away.
5. Enjoy!

NUTRITION: Calories 300 Fat 4g Carbs 26g Protein 34g

DIABETICS AIR FRYER VEGETABLES

128. Mushrooms Marinated In Garlic Coco-aminos

Preparation Time: 10 minutes
Cooking Time: 20 minutes
Servings: 8
INGREDIENTS:
- 1/4 cup coconut aminos
- 2 cloves of garlic, minced
- 2 pounds mushrooms, sliced
- 3 tablespoons olive oil

DIRECTIONS:
1. Place all ingredients in a dish and mix until well-combined.
2. Allow to marinate for hours in the fridge.
3. Preheat the air fryer for 5 minutes.
4. Place the mushrooms in a heat-proof dish that will fit in the air fryer.
5. Cook for 20 minutes at 30 degrees F.

NUTRITION: Calories: 77 Fat: 7g Carbs: 4g Protein: 0.8g

129. Potato Filled Bread Rolls

Preparation Time: 10 minutes
Cooking Time: 25 minutes
Servings: 4
INGREDIENTS:
- 5 large potatoes, boiled and mashed
- 1/2 tsp turmeric
- 2 green chilies, deseeded and chopped
- 1 medium onion, finely chopped
- 1/2 tsp mustard seeds
- 1 tbsp olive oil
- 2 sprigs curry leaf
- Salt to taste

DIRECTIONS:
1. Preheat air fryer to 350 F.
2. Combine olive oil, onion, curry leaves, and mustard seed in a baking dish.
3. Add in the air fryer basket and cook for 5 minutes. Mix the onion mixture with the mashed potatoes, chilies, turmeric, and salt.
4. Divide the mixture into 8 equal pieces. Trim the sides of the bread, and wet with some water. Make sure to get rid of the excess water.
5. Take one wet bread slice in your palm and place one of the potato pieces in the center.
6. Roll the bread over the filling, sealing the edges. Place the rolls onto a prepared baking dish, and air fry for 12 minutes.

NUTRITION: Calories: 93 Fat: 1g Carbs: 16g Protein: 4g

130. Elegant Garlic Mushroom

Preparation Time:
Cooking Time: 20 minutes
Servings: 3
INGREDIENTS:
- 2 tbsp vermouth
- 1/2 tsp garlic powder
- 1 tbsp olive oil
- 2 tsp herbs
- 1 tbsp duck fat

DIRECTIONS:
1. Preheat your air fryer to 350 F, add duck fat, garlic powder and herbs in a blender, and process.
2. Pour the mixture over the mushrooms and cover with vermouth.
3. Place the mushrooms in the cooking basket and cook for minutes.
4. Top with more vermouth and cook for 5 more minutes.

NUTRITION: Calories: 83 Fat: 7g Carbs: 4g Protein: 4g

131. Rosemary Au Gratin Potatoes

Preparation Time: 10 minutes
Cooking Time: 45 minutes
Servings: 4
INGREDIENTS:
- 2 pounds potatoes

- 1/4 cup sunflower kernels, soaked overnight
- 1/2 cup almonds, soaked overnight
- 1 cup unsweetened almond milk
- 2 tablespoons nutritional yeast
- 1 teaspoon shallot powder
- 2 fresh garlic cloves, minced
- 1/2 cup water
- Kosher salt
- Ground black pepper, to taste
- 1 teaspoon cayenne pepper
- 1 tablespoon fresh rosemary

DIRECTIONS:
1. Prepare a large pan of water to a boil. Cook the whole potatoes for about 20 minutes. Drain the potatoes and let sit until cool enough to handle.
2. Peel your potatoes and slice into 1/8-inch rounds.
3. Add the sunflower kernels, almonds, almond milk, nutritional yeast, shallot powder, and garlic to your food processor, blend until uniform, smooth, and creamy.
4. Add the water and blend for seconds more.
5. Place 1/2 of the potatoes overlapping in a single layer in the lightly greased casserole dish. Spoon 1/2 of the sauce on top of the potatoes. Repeat the layers, ending with the sauce.
6. Top with salt, black pepper, cayenne pepper, and fresh rosemary. Bake in the preheated Air Fryer at 320 degrees F for 20 minutes. Serve warm.

NUTRITION: Calories: 100 Fat: 0.5g Carbs: 21g Protein: 2g

132. Three Veg Bake

Preparation Time: 19 minutes
Cooking Time: 30 minutes
Servings: 3
INGREDIENTS:
- 1 large red onion, cut into rings
- 1 large zucchini, sliced
- Salt and pepper to taste
- 2 cloves garlic, crushed
- 1 bay leaf, cut in 6 pieces
- 1 tbsp olive oil

- Cooking spray

DIRECTIONS:
1. Place the turnips, onion, and zucchini in a bowl. Toss with olive oil and season with salt and pepper.
2. Preheat the air fryer to 330 F and place the veggies into a baking pan that fits the air fryer.
3. Slip the bay leaves in the slices' different parts and tuck the garlic cloves in between the slices.
4. Insert the pan in the air fryer's basket and cook for 15 minutes.
5. Serve warm with salad.

NUTRITION: Calories: 158 Fat: 5g Carbs: 18g Protein: 9g

133. Garden Fresh Green Beans

Preparation Time: 10 minutes
Cooking Time: 12 minutes
Servings: 4
INGREDIENTS:
- 1-pound green beans, washed and trimmed
- 1 teaspoon butter, melted
- 1 tablespoon fresh lemon juice
- 1/4 teaspoon garlic powder
- Salt and freshly ground pepper, to taste

DIRECTIONS:
1. Preheat the Air fryer to 400 F and grease an Air fryer basket.
2. Put all the ingredients in a large bowl and transfer into the Air fryer basket.
3. Cook for about 8 minutes and dish out in a bowl to serve warm.

NUTRITION: Calories: 75 Fat: 3g Carbs: 12g Protein: 3g

134. Tofu In Sweet & Spicy Sauce

Preparation Time: 10 minutes
Cooking Time: 25 minutes
Servings: 3
INGREDIENTS:
- For Tofu:
- 1 (14-ounces) block firm tofu, pressed and cubed

- 1/2 cup arrowroot flour
- 1/2 teaspoon sesame oil
- For Sauce:
- 4 tablespoons low-sodium soy sauce
- 11/2 tablespoons rice vinegar
- 11/2 tablespoons chili sauce
- 1 tablespoon agave nectar
- 2 large garlic cloves, minced
- 1 teaspoon fresh ginger, peeled and grated
- 2 scallions (green part), chopped

DIRECTIONS:
1. In a bowl, mix together the tofu, arrowroot flour, and sesame oil.
2. Set the temperature of air fryer to 360 degrees F. Generously, grease an air fryer basket.
3. Arrange tofu pieces into the prepared air fryer basket in a single layer.
4. Air fry for about 20 minutes, shaking once halfway through.
5. Meanwhile, for the sauce: in a bowl, add all the ingredients except scallions and beat until well combined.
6. Remove from air fryer and transfer the tofu into a skillet with sauce over medium heat and cook for about 3 minutes, stirring occasionally.
7. Garnish with scallions and serve hot.

NUTRITION: Calories: 250 Fat: 8g Carbs: 32g Protein: 15g

135. Fried Broccoli From India

Preparation Time: 10 minutes
Cooking Time: 15 minutes
Servings: 6
INGREDIENTS:
- 1/4 teaspoon turmeric powder
- 1/2 pounds broccoli, cut into florets
- 1 tablespoon almond flour
- 1 teaspoon garam masala
- 2 tablespoons coconut milk
- Salt and pepper to taste

DIRECTIONS:
1. Preheat the air fryer for 5 minutes.
2. In a bowl, combine all ingredients until the broccoli florets are coated with the other ingredients.

3. Place in a fryer basket and cook for 15 minutes until crispy.

NUTRITION: Calories: 114 Fat: 5g Carbs: 14g Protein: 6g

136. Cheesy Kale

Preparation Time: 10 minutes
Cooking Time: 15 minutes
Servings: 2
INGREDIENTS:
- 1/2 lb. kale
- 8 oz. parmesan cheese, shredded
- 1 onion, diced
- 1 tsp. butter
- 1 cup heavy cream

DIRECTIONS:
1. Dice up the kale, discarding any hard stems.
2. Get a small baking dish enough to fit inside the fryer, combine the kale with the parmesan, onion, butter, and cream.
3. Pre-heat the fryer at 390°F.
4. Set the baking dish in the fryer and cook for twelve minutes. Make sure to give it a good stir before serving.

NUTRITION: Calories: 95 Fat: 4g Carbs: 12g Protein: 5g

137. Baked Potato Topped With Cream Cheese and Olives

Preparation Time:
Cooking Time: 40 minutes
Servings: 1
INGREDIENTS:
- 1/4 teaspoon onion powder
- 1 medium russet potato, scrubbed and peeled
- 1 tablespoon chives, chopped
- 1 tablespoon Kalamata olives
- 1 teaspoon olive oil
- 1/8 teaspoon salt
- a dollop of vegan butter
- a dollop of vegan cream cheese

DIRECTIONS:

1. Place inside the air fryer basket and cook for 40 minutes. Be sure to turn the potatoes once halfway.
2. Place the potatoes in a mixing bowl and pour olive oil, onion powder, salt, and vegan butter.
3. Preheat the air fryer to 400 F.
4. Serve the potatoes with vegan cream cheese, Kalamata olives, chives, and other vegan toppings that you want.

NUTRITION: Calories: 145 Fat: 1g Carbs: 31g Protein: 5g

138. Spices Stuffed Eggplants

Preparation Time: 10 minutes
Cooking Time: 12 minutes
Servings: 4
INGREDIENTS:
- 8 baby eggplants
- 4 teaspoons olive oil, divided
- 3/4 tablespoon dry mango powder
- 3/4 tablespoon ground coriander
- 1/2 teaspoon ground cumin
- 1/2 teaspoon ground turmeric
- 1/2 teaspoon garlic powder
- Salt, to taste

DIRECTIONS:
1. Preheat the Air fryer to 370 o F and grease an Air fryer basket.
2. Make slits from the bottom of each eggplant leaving the stems intact.
3. Mix one teaspoon of oil and spices in a bowl and fill each slit of eggplants with this mixture.
4. Brush each eggplant's outer side with remaining oil and arrange in the Air fryer basket.
5. Cook for about 12 minutes and dish out in a serving plate to serve hot.

NUTRITION: Calories: 106 Fat: 3g Carbs: 20g Protein: 3g

139. Pull-apart Bread With Garlic Oil

Preparation Time: 10 minutes
Cooking Time: 10 minutes
Servings: 2

DIABETICS AIR FRYER VEGETABLES

INGREDIENTS:
- 1 large vegan bread loaf
- 2 tablespoons garlic puree
- 2 tablespoons nutritional yeast
- 2 tablespoons olive oil
- 2 teaspoons chives
- salt and pepper to taste

DIRECTIONS:
1. Preheat the air fryer to 3570F.
2. Slice the bread loaf making sure that you don't slice through the bread.
3. In a mixing bowl, combine the olive oil, garlic puree, and nutritional yeast.
4. Pour over the mixture on top of the slices you made on the bread.
5. Sprinkle with chopped chives and season with salt and pepper.
6. Place inside the air fryer and cook for 10 minutes or until the garlic is thoroughly cooked.

NUTRITION: Calories: 51 Fat: 6g Carbs: 1g Protein: 1g

140. Chickpeas & Spinach With Coconut

Preparation Time: 15 minutes
Cooking Time: 20 minutes
Servings: 4
INGREDIENTS:
- 1 tbsp pepper
- 1 onion, chopped
- 1 tsp salt
- 4 garlic cloves, minced
- 1 can coconut milk
- 1 tbsp ginger, minced
- 1-pound spinach
- 1/2 cup dried tomatoes, chopped
- 1 can chickpeas
- 1 lemon, juiced
- 1 hot pepper

DIRECTIONS:
1. Preheat air fryer to 370 F.
2. In a bowl, mix lemon juice, tomatoes, pepper, ginger, coconut milk, garlic, salt, hot pepper, and onion.
3. Rinse chickpeas under running water to get rid of all the gunk.

4. Put them in a large bowl. Cover with spinach.
5. Pour the sauce over and stir in oil. Cook in the air fryer for 15 minutes. Serve warm.

NUTRITION: Calories: 124 Fat: 4g Carbs: 17g Protein: 5g

141. Lemony Green Beans

Preparation Time: 10 minutes
Cooking Time: 12 minutes
Servings: 3
INGREDIENTS:

- 1-pound green beans, trimmed and halved
- 1 teaspoon butter, melted
- 1 tablespoon fresh lemon juice
- 1/4 teaspoon garlic powder

DIRECTIONS:

1. Preheat the Air fryer to 400 o F and grease an Air fryer basket.
2. Mix all the ingredients in a bowl and toss to coat well.
3. Arrange the green beans into the Air fryer basket and cook for about 12 minutes.
4. Dish out in a serving plate and serve hot.

NUTRITION: Calories: 60 Fat: 3g Carbs: 7g Protein: 2g

142. Creole Seasoned Vegetables

Preparation Time: 10 minutes
Cooking Time: 15 minutes
Servings: 5
INGREDIENTS:

- 1/4 cup honey
- 1/4 cup yellow mustard
- 1 large red bell pepper, sliced
- 1 teaspoon black pepper
- 1 teaspoon salt
- 2 large yellow squash, cut into 1/2-inch-thick slices
- 2 medium zucchinis, cut into 1/2-inch-thick slices
- 2 teaspoons creole seasoning
- 2 teaspoons smoked paprika
- 3 tablespoons olive oil

DIRECTIONS:

DIABETICS AIR FRYER VEGETABLES

1. Preheat the air fryer to 330 F.
2. Place the grill pan accessory in the air fryer.
3. In a Ziploc bag, put the zucchini, squash, red bell pepper, olive oil, salt, and pepper. Give a shake to season all vegetables.
4. Set the grill pan and cook for 15 minutes.
5. Meanwhile, prepare the sauce by combining the mustard, honey, paprika, and creole seasoning. Season with salt to taste.
6. Serve the vegetables with the sauce.

NUTRITION: Calories: 35 Fat: 2g Carbs: 3g Protein: 1.4g

143. Saltine Wax Beans

Preparation Time: 10 minutes
Cooking Time: 7 minutes
Servings: 4
INGREDIENTS:

- 1/2 cup flour
- 1 teaspoon smoky chipotle powder
- 1/2 teaspoon ground black pepper
- 1 teaspoon sea salt flakes
- 2 eggs, beaten
- 1/2 cup crushed saltines
- 10 ounces (283 g) wax beans
- Cooking spray

DIRECTIONS:

1. Preheat the air fryer oven to 360F (182C).
2. Combine the flour, chipotle powder, black pepper, and salt in a bowl. Put the eggs in second bowl. Put the crushed saltines in third bowl.
3. Wash the beans with cold water and discard any tough strings.
4. Coat the beans with the flour mixture before dipping them into the beaten egg. Cover them with the crushed saltines.
5. Spritz the beans with cooking spray, then transfer to the air fryer basket.
6. Move the baking pan to the fryer basket and set time to 4 minutes.
7. Give the air fryer basket a good shake and continue to air fry for 3 minutes. Serve hot.

NUTRITION: Calories: 35 Fiber: 3g Carbs: 7g Protein: 2g

144. Easy Rosemary Green Beans

Preparation Time: 5 minutes
Cooking Time: 5 minutes
Servings: 1
INGREDIENTS:
- 1 tablespoon butter, melted
- 2 tablespoons rosemary
- 1/2 teaspoon salt
- 3 cloves garlic, minced
- 3/4 cup chopped green beans

DIRECTIONS:
1. Preheat the air fryer oven to 390F (199C).
2. Combine the melted butter with the rosemary, salt, and minced garlic.
3. Toss in the green beans, coating them well. Transfer to the air fryer basket. Set air fryer time to 5 minutes.
4. Serve immediately.

NUTRITION: Calories: 32 Fat: 0.3g Carbs: 8g Protein: 2g

145. Sriracha Golden Cauliflower

Preparation Time: 5 minutes
Cooking Time: 17 minutes
Servings: 4
INGREDIENTS:
- 1/4 cup vegan butter, melted
- 1/4 cup sriracha sauce
- 4 cups cauliflower florets
- 1 cup breadcrumbs
- 1 teaspoon salt

DIRECTIONS:
1. Preheat the air fryer oven to 375F (191C).
2. Mix the sriracha and vegan butter in a bowl and pour this mixture over the cauliflower, taking care to cover each floret entirely.
3. Get another bowl. Mix the breadcrumbs and salt.
4. Dip the cauliflower florets in the breadcrumbs, coating each one well. Put them in the air fryer basket and set time to 17 minutes. Serve hot.

NUTRITION: Calories: 469 Fat: 34g Carbs: 35g Protein: 15g

146. Cauliflower Tater Tots

Preparation Time: 15 minutes
Cooking Time: 16 minutes
SERVINGS: 12
INGREDIENTS:
- 1pound (454 g) cauliflower, steamed and chopped
- 1/2 cup Nutritional yeast
- 1 tablespoon oats
- 1 tablespoon desiccated coconuts
- 3 tablespoons flaxseed meal
- 3 tablespoons water
- 1 onion, chopped
- 1 teaspoon minced garlic
- 1 teaspoon chopped parsley
- 1 teaspoon chopped oregano
- 1 teaspoon chopped chives
- Salt and ground black pepper, to taste
- 1/2 cup breadcrumbs

DIRECTIONS:
1. Preheat the air fryer oven to 390F (199C).
2. Drain any excess water out of the cauliflower by wringing it with a paper towel.
3. Mix the cauliflower with the remaining ingredients, save the breadcrumbs. Using the hands, shape the mixture into several small balls.
4. Coat the balls in the breadcrumbs and transfer to the air fryer
5. Change temperature to 400 degrees F and air fry for an additional 10 minutes.
6. Serve immediately.

NUTRITION: Calories: 147 Fat: 6g Carbs: 20g Protein: 3g

147. Chili Fingerling Potatoes

Preparation Time: 10 minutes
Cooking Time: 16 minutes
Servings: 4
INGREDIENTS:
- 1pound fingerling potatoes, rinsed and cut into wedges
- 1 teaspoon olive oil
- 1 teaspoon salt
- 1 teaspoon black pepper

- 1 teaspoon cayenne pepper
- 1 teaspoon Nutritional yeast
- 1/2 teaspoon garlic powder

DIRECTIONS:
1. Preheat the air fryer oven to 400F (204C).
2. Coat the potatoes with the rest of the ingredients. Transfer to the air fryer basket.
3. Place in the air fryer basket set time to 16 minutes, shaking the basket halfway through the cooking time.
4. Serve immediately.

NUTRITION: Calories: 120 Fat: 4g Carbs: 20g Protein: 2.4g

148. Potato with Creamy Cheese

Preparation Time: 5 minutes
Cooking Time: 15 minutes
Servings: 2
INGREDIENTS:
- 2 medium potatoes
- 1 teaspoon butter
- 3 tablespoons sour cream
- 1 teaspoon chives
- 1 1/2 tablespoons grated Parmesan cheese

DIRECTIONS:
1. Preheat the air fryer oven to 350 degrees F.
2. Stick the potatoes with a fork and boil them in water until they are cooked. Move to the air fryer basket and cook for 15 minutes.
3. In the meantime, combine the sour cream, cheese, and chives in bowl.
4. Cut the potatoes halfway to open them up and fill with the butter and sour cream mixture.
5. Serve immediately.

NUTRITION: Calories: 184 Fat: 2g Carbs: 38g Protein: 5g

149. Golden Pickles

Preparation Time: 10 minutes
Cooking Time: 15 minutes
Servings: 4
INGREDIENTS:
- 14 dill pickles, sliced
- 1/4 cup flour

- 1/8 teaspoon baking powder
- Pinch of salt
- 2 tablespoons cornstarch plus 3 tablespoons water
- 6 tablespoons panko breadcrumbs
- 1/2 teaspoon paprika
- Cooking spray

DIRECTIONS:
1. Preheat the air fryer oven to 400F (204C).
2. Drain any excess moisture out of the dill pickles on paper towel.
3. In bowl, combine the flour, baking powder, and salt.
4. Throw in the cornstarch and water mixture and combine well with a whisk.
5. Put the panko breadcrumbs in shallow dish along with the paprika. Mix thoroughly.
6. Dip the pickles in the flour batter before coating in the breadcrumbs. Spritz all the pickles with the cooking spray.
7. Transfer to the air fryer basket. Choose Air Fry and set time to 15 minutes, or until golden brown. Serve immediately.

NUTRITION: Calories: 195 Fat: 13g Carbs: 20g Protein: 26g

150. Garlic Eggplant Slices

Preparation Time: 5 minutes
Cooking Time: 15 minutes
Servings: 1
INGREDIENTS:
- 1 large eggplant, sliced
- 2 tablespoons olive oil
- 1/4 teaspoon salt
- 1/2 teaspoon garlic powder

DIRECTIONS:
1. Preheat the air fryer oven to 390F (199C).
2. Put eggplant slices with the olive oil, salt, and garlic powder in a mixing bowl until evenly coated.
3. Put the slices in the air fryer basket. Place the baking pan and cook for 15 minutes.
4. Serve immediately.

NUTRITION: Calories: 66 Fat: 7g Carbs: 1g

151. Zucchini Balls

Preparation Time: 5 minutes

Cooking Time: 10 minutes
Servings: 4
INGREDIENTS:

- 4 zucchinis
- 1 egg
- 1/2 cup grated Parmesan cheese
- 1 tablespoon Italian herbs
- 1 cup grated coconut

DIRECTIONS:

1. Thinly grate the zucchinis and dry with a cheesecloth, ensuring to remove all the moisture.
2. Blend and mix well zucchinis with the egg, Parmesan, Italian herbs, and grated coconut in a bowl.
3. Form the mixture into balls.
4. Preheat the air fryer oven to 400F (204C).
5. Lay the zucchini balls in the air fryer basket and cook for 10 minutes.
6. Serve hot.

NUTRITION: Calories: 105 Fat: 3g Carbs: 16g Protein: 6g

152. Lemony Falafel

Preparation Time: 10 minutes
Cooking Time: 15 minutes
Servings: 8
INGREDIENTS:

- 1 teaspoon cumin seeds
- 1/2 teaspoon coriander seeds
- 2 cups chickpeas, drained and rinsed
- 1/2 teaspoon red pepper flakes
- 3 cloves garlic
- 1/4 cup chopped parsley
- 1/4 cup chopped coriander
- 1/2 onion, diced
- 1 tablespoon juice from freshly squeezed lemon
- 3 tablespoons flour
- 1/2 teaspoon salt
- Cooking spray

DIRECTIONS:

1. Cook the cumin and coriander seeds over medium heat.
2. Grind using a mortar and pestle.

3. Put all ingredients, except for the cooking spray, in a food processor and blend until a fine consistency is achieved.
4. Use the hands to mold the mixture into falafels and spritz with the cooking spray.
5. Preheat the air fryer oven to 400F (204C).
6. Transfer the falafels to the air fryer basket in a single layer. Cook until golden brown. Serve warm.

NUTRITION: Calories: 56 Fat: 1g Carbs: 9g Protein: 3g

153. Sweet and Sour Tofu

Preparation Time: 15 minutes
Cooking Time: 20 minutes
Servings: 2
INGREDIENTS:

- 2 teaspoons apple cider vinegar
- 1 tablespoon sugar
- 1 tablespoon soy sauce
- 3 teaspoons lime juice
- 1 teaspoon ground ginger
- 1 teaspoon garlic powder
- 1/2 block firm tofu pressed to remove excess liquid and cut into cubes
- 1 teaspoon cornstarch
- 2 green onions, chopped
- Toasted sesame seeds, for garnish

DIRECTIONS:

1. In bowl, thoroughly combine the apple cider vinegar, sugar, soy sauce, lime juice, ground ginger, and garlic powder.
2. Cover the tofu with this mixture and leave to marinate for at least 30 minutes.
3. Preheat the air fryer oven to 400F (204C).
4. Move the tofu to the air fryer basket, keeping any excess marinade for the sauce.
5. Cook the tofu for 20 minutes, or until crispy.
6. In the meantime, thicken the sauce with the cornstarch over medium low heat.
7. Serve the cooked tofu with the sauce, green onions, and sesame seeds.

NUTRITION: Calories: 207 Fat: 11g Carbs: 13g Protein: 18g

154. Crispy Chickpeas

Preparation Time: 5 minutes
Cooking Time: 15 minutes
Servings: 4
INGREDIENTS:

- 1 can (15ounces / 425g) chickpeas, drained but not rinsed
- 2 tablespoons olive oil
- 1 teaspoon salt
- 2 tablespoons lemon juice

DIRECTIONS:

DIABETICS AIR FRYER VEGETABLES

1. Preheat the air fryer oven to 400F (204C).
2. Put and mix all ingredients in a bowl. Transfer this mixture to the air fryer basket.
3. Put mixture into baking pan and slide into Rack Position 2, select Air Fry, and set time to 15 minutes, ensuring the chickpeas become nice and crispy.
4. Serve immediately.

NUTRITION: Calories: 132 Fat: 6g Carbs: 14g Protein: 5g

DIABETICS AIR FRYER SOUPS AND STEWS

155. Teriyaki Beef Stew

Preparation Time: 20 minutes
Cooking Time: 30 minutes
Servings: 8
INGREDIENTS:
- 2 Garlic cloves, minced
- 2 Tbsp. sesame seeds
- 2 Tbsp. cornstarch
- 2 Lbs. beef stew meat (browned)
- 1 Bottle (12 Oz.) ginger beer
- 1/4 Cup of teriyaki sauce
- 2 Tbsp. cold water
- 2 Cups of frozen peas, thawed

DIRECTIONS:
1. Preheat the Air Fryer to 375 F. Merge teriyaki sauce, ginger beer, and garlic and sesame seeds in a small mixing bowl.
2. Pour the mixture on the cooked beef. Merge cornstarch and cold water and give it a nice mix.
3. Turn it into the stew, stir and add peas. Place in the Air Fryer and cook for 30 minutes.
4. Serve and enjoy!

NUTRITION: Calories: 175 Fat: 0g Carbs: 22g Protein: 4g

156. Sweet Potato Lentil Stew

Preparation Time: 10 minutes
Cooking Time: 30 minutes
Servings: 6
INGREDIENTS:
- 1/2 Tsp. ground cumin
- 1/4 Tsp. ground ginger
- 1/4 Tsp. cayenne pepper
- 1 1/4 Lb. sweet potatoes cut into pieces
- 1 1/2 Cups dried lentils, rinsed
- 3 medium carrots, cut into pieces
- 1 medium onion, chopped
- 4 garlic cloves, minced
- 1 Carton of vegetable broth
- 1/4 Cup of minced fresh cilantro

DIRECTIONS:
1. Ready the Air Fryer to 400 degrees F.
2. Merge the first 9 ingredients.
3. Prepare in the fryer basket and cook for at least 30 minutes.
4. Top with cilantro.
5. Serve and enjoy!

NUTRITION: Calories: 116 Fat: 1g Carbs: 23g Protein: 4g

157. Fall Stew

Preparation Time: 15 minutes
Cooking Time: 20 minutes
Servings: 4
Calories: 483 kcal
INGREDIENTS:
- 2 Medium carrots
- 2 Ribs of celery, chopped
- 2 Tsp. Worcestershire sauce
- 1 Bay leaf
- 6 Cups vegetable broth
- 2 Lbs. beef stew meat, cut
- 1 Tsp. sea salt
- 1/2 Tsp. Black pepper
- 1/2 Tsp. Onion powder
- 1/2 Tsp. Chili powder
- 2 1/2 Tsp. Italian seasoning, divided
- 1 Medium onion
- 4 Garlic cloves, minced
- 6 Tbsp. tomato paste
- 2 Tbsp. balsamic vinegar
- 4 Medium russet potatoes, peeled and chopped
- 1/2 Cup of corn
- 1 Can of chickpeas

DIRECTIONS:
1. Peel and cut carrots into slices.
2. Preheat the Air Fryer to 400 F. Merge beef, salt, pepper, onion powder, chili powder, and 1/2 Tsp. of Italian seasoning.
3. Place them in the Air Fryer together with the remaining ingredients.
4. Cook at 375 F for at least 20 minutes.

5. Serve and enjoy!
NUTRITION: Calories: 360 Fat: 6g Carbs: 32g Protein: 44g

158. Manchester Stew

Preparation Time: 10 minutes
Cooking Time: 30 minutes
Servings: 6
INGREDIENTS:
- 2 1/2 Cups of water
- 1 Can no-salt-added diced tomatoes
- 1 Tsp. dried thyme
- 1/2 Tsp. salt
- 2 Tbsp. olive oil
- 2 Medium onions, chopped
- 2 Garlic cloves, minced
- 1 Tsp. dried oregano
- 1 Cup of dry red wine
- 1 Lb. small red potatoes, quartered
- 1 Can kidney beans, rinsed and drained
- 1/2 Lb. sliced fresh mushrooms
- 2 Medium leeks (white portion only), sliced
- 1 Cup of fresh baby carrots

DIRECTIONS:
1. Preheat the Air Fryer to 400 F. Merge garlic, onions, oil, oregano, and wine into the Air Fryer.
2. Put potatoes, beans, mushrooms, leeks and carrots, water, tomatoes, thyme, salt, and pepper.
3. Cook for at least 30 minutes. Top with fresh basil.
4. Serve and enjoy!

NUTRITION: Calories: 220 Fat: 1g Carbs: 30g Protein: 8g

159. Tuscan Pork Stew

Preparation Time: 10 minutes
Cooking Time: 30 minutes
Servings: 8
INGREDIENTS:
- 2 Garlic cloves, minced
- 1 Tsp. dried oregano
- 1/2 Tsp. fennel seed
- 1/2 Tsp. pepper

- 1 1/2 Lb. boneless pork loin roast, cut into cubes (browned)
- 2 Tbsp. olive oil
- 2 Cans Italian diced tomatoes, undrained
- 2 Cups of chicken broth
- 2 Cups of frozen pepper stir-fry vegetable blend, thawed
- 1/2 Cup of dry red wine
- 1/4 Cup orange marmalade
- 2 Tbsp. cornstarch
- 2 Tbsp. cold water

DIRECTIONS:
1. Preheat the Air Fryer to 400 F. In a small mixing bowl, merge pork, tomatoes, broth, vegetable blend, and wine.
2. Add the marmalade, garlic, oregano, fennel seed, and pepper. Place in the Air Fryer and stir in cook for at least 30 minutes.
3. Merge cornstarch and water. Mix well and stir into the stew. Cook in the Air Fryer for about 30 minutes.
4. Serve and enjoy!

NUTRITION: Calories: 235 Fat: 7g Carbs: 20g Protein: 18g

160. Southwest Turkey Stew

Preparation Time: 15 minutes
Cooking Time: 30 minutes
Servings: 6
INGREDIENTS:
- 1 1/2 Lb. turkey breast tenderloins, cubed
- 2 Tsp. canola oil
- 1 Can turkey chili with beans, undrained
- 1 Can diced tomatoes, undrained
- 1 Medium sweet red pepper, chopped
- 1 Medium green pepper, chopped
- 3/4 Cup of chopped onion
- 3/4 Cup of salsa
- 3 Garlic cloves, minced
- 1 1/2 Tsp. chili powder
- 1/2 Tsp. ground cumin
- 1/4 Tsp. salt

DIRECTIONS:
1. Preheat the Air Fryer to 375 F. In a small mixing bowl, merge turkey, chili, tomatoes,

peppers, onion, salsa, garlic, chili powder, cumin, and salt.
2. Place in the Air Fryer basket and cook for about 30 minutes.
3. Serve and enjoy!!!

NUTRITION: Calories: 238 Fat: 4g Carbs: 17 g Protein: 30g

161. Tomato Black Bean Soup

Preparation Time: 20 minutes
Cooking Time: 25 minutes
Servings: 6
INGREDIENTS:

- Soup:
- 1/2 Medium white onion chopped
- 2 Tbsp. corn oil
- 4 Cups of cooked black beans - puréed
- 3 Roma tomatoes, chopped
- 1 Ancho chile, stemmed and seeded
- 1 1/2 Cups of water
- 3 Cloves garlic
- 2 1/2 Cups of vegetable broth
- 1 Tsp. salt
- Toppings:
- Tortilla chips or strips
- Chopped ripe Hass avocado
- Fried ancho chile strips
- Vegan sour cream

DIRECTIONS:
1. Preheat the Air Fryer to 400 F. Merge tomatoes, ancho, garlic, onion, and water in a small mixing bowl. Put in a blender and blend properly.
2. Sprinkle oil on the Air Fryer basket. Put the blended mixture and cook for about 5 minutes. Put the pureed beans, vegetable broth, and salt.
3. Cook for another 10 minutes. Top with any topping of your choice.
4. Serve and enjoy!

NUTRITION: Calories: 134 Fat: 1g Carbs: 24g Protein: 7g

162. Beefy Cabbage Bean Stew

Preparation Time: 20 minutes

Cooking Time: 30 minutes
Servings: 6
INGREDIENTS:

- 1 Medium green pepper, chopped
- 1 Small onion, chopped
- 3 Garlic cloves, minced
- 1/2 Lb. lean ground beef
- 3 Cups of shredded cabbage
- 1 Can red beans, rinsed and drained
- 1 Can diced tomatoes, undrained
- 1 Can (8 Oz.) tomato sauce
- 3/4 Cup of salsa or picante sauce
- 1 Tsp. ground cumin
- 1/2 Tsp. pepper

DIRECTIONS:
1. Preheat the Air Fryer to 400F.
2. Merge all the ingredients into the Air Fryer and cook for about 30 minutes.
3. Serve and enjoy!

NUTRITION: Calories: 177 Fat: 4g Carbs: 23g Protein: 13g

163. Spicy Chicken Stew

Preparation Time: 10 minutes
Cooking Time: 15 minutes
Servings: 6
INGREDIENTS:

- 1 Can garbanzo beans rinsed and drained
- 1 Can diced tomatoes with onions, undrained
- 1 Cup lime-garlic salsa
- 2 Lbs. boneless skinless chicken thighs, cut into pieces
- 2 Tsp. minced garlic
- 2 Tbsp. olive oil
- 1 Tsp. ground cumin
- 1/3 Cup of minced fresh cilantro

DIRECTIONS:
1. Preheat the Air Fryer to 400 F. In a small mixing bowl, merge chicken, garlic, beans, tomatoes, cilantro, salsa, and cumin.
2. Place them in the Air Fryer basket and cook for at least 15 minutes.
3. Serve and enjoy!

NUTRITION: Calories: 250 Fat: 6g Carbs: 30g Protein: 17g

164. Apple Chicken Stew

Preparation Time: 15 minutes
Cooking Time: 35 minutes
Servings: 8
INGREDIENTS:

- 1 1/2 Tsp. salt
- 3/4 Tsp. dried thyme
- 1/2 Tsp. pepper
- 2 Tbsp. olive oil
- 1 Bay leaf
- 1 Large tart apple
- 1/2 Tsp. caraway seeds
- 1 Tbsp. cider vinegar
- 1 1/2 Lb. potatoes, cut into pieces
- 4 Medium carrots, cut into slices
- 1 Medium red onion, halved and sliced
- 1 Celery rib, thinly sliced
- 2 Lb. boneless skinless chicken breasts, cut into pieces
- 1 1/4 Cups apple cider
- Minced fresh parsley

DIRECTIONS:

1. Peel and cut tar apple into cubes
2. Warm the Air Fryer to 400 F. In a small mixing bowl, merge the first 4 ingredients.
3. Layer vegetables in the Air Fryer basket alongside with half of the mixture in the bowl.
4. Place the chicken in the Air Fryer and top with bay leaf, apple, vinegar, and cider.
5. Cook for at least 35 minutes. Garnish with parsley.
6. Serve and enjoy!

NUTRITION: Calories: 280 Fat: 6g Carbs: 30g Protein: 26 g

165. Tomato and Vegetable Soup

Preparation Time: 10 minutes
Cooking Time: 5 minutes
Servings: 4
INGREDIENTS:

- 2 Tbsp. olive oil
- 2 Vegetable bouillon cubes
- Water

- 800g Tomatoes, chopped
- 1 Onion
- 1 Leek, cut into rings
- 50g Peas
- 100g Vermicelli
- 1 Container cherry tomatoes, halved
- 1 Tbsp. celery, chopped

DIRECTIONS:

1. Preheat the Air Fryer to 400 F.
2. Get a mixing bowl, combine the tomatoes, olive oil, and onion.
3. Add the peas, celery, leeks, halved cherry tomatoes, bouillon cubes, vermicelli, and water.
4. Place in the fryer and cook for about 5 minutes. Make fresh bread available.
5. Serve and enjoy!!

NUTRITION: Calories: 53 Fat: 0.8g Carbs: 10g Protein: 2g

166. Tomato Basil Soup

Preparation Time: 10 minutes
Cooking Time: 25 minutes
Servings: 4
INGREDIENTS:

- 4 Garlic cloves peeled
- 1/2 Cups chicken broth
- 1/2 Cup heavy cream
- 1/2 tsp. Oil
- 1 Lb. red tomatoes cut in half
- 1 Red bell pepper quartered
- 1 Yellow onion quartered
- 1 Carrot chopped
- 4 Fresh basil leaves chopped
- Splash of balsamic vinegar

DIRECTIONS:

1. Preheat the Air Fryer to 4000F. Pour some oil on the Air Fryer cooking basket. Put the tomatoes, red bell pepper, onion, carrot, garlic cloves to the Air Fryer.
2. Cook at 3600F for about 25 minutes. Shaking halfway through for proper cooking. Flip the vegetables onto a medium pan and place chicken broth.
3. Bring the mixture to a boil. Simmer for at least 5 minutes. Add the soup to an immersion blender and blend properly.

4. Put basil, heavy cream, balsamic vinegar, Salt, and pepper. Top with parmesan cheese.
5. Serve and enjoy!!!

NUTRITION: Calories: 150 Fat: 10g Carbs: 14 g Protein: 2g

167. Hot Chili Soup

Preparation Time: 10 minutes
Cooking Time: 15 – 20 minutes
Servings: 4
INGREDIENTS:

- 2 tbsp olive oil
- 2 pieces of chili peppers fresh
- 360 ml chicken broth
- 360 ml water
- 1/2 tsp Ground cumin
- 32 g tomato paste
- 350 g chicken meat
- 30 g butter
- 1 avocado
- 60 g cream cheese
- 15 ml lime juice
- salt
- pepper

DIRECTIONS:

1. Core chili peppers and cut into small pieces.
2. Cut the chicken into small pieces.
3. Coat an air fryer with olive oil and sauté the meat and set aside.
4. Heat 2 tbsp of olive oil in air fryer, add the coriander seeds and wait until they develop their aroma.
5. Do all pieces of chili peppers.
6. Add chicken stock and water into the pot and let it boil.
7. Season with cumin, salt, and pepper.
8. Bring the soup to a boil briefly.
9. Then stir in the tomato paste and butter.
10. Now simmer the soup for another 5 to 10 minutes. Add lime juice.
11. Put 1/4 of the meat in a soup plate (or bowl), fill with soup and refine with 1 spoon of cream cheese. Garnish with coriander.
12. If necessary, season with salt and pepper.

13. Slice the avocado and place 1/4 of each in a soup plate.

NUTRITION: Calories: 199 Fat: 2g Carbs: 24g Protein: 21g

168. Paprika Cauliflower Soup

Preparation Time: 10 minutes
Cooking Time:
Servings: 4
INGREDIENTS:

- 360 g bell peppers, red or green
- 320 g cauliflower
- 23 g olive oil
- 18 g spring onion
- 4 g garlic
- 90 g feta
- 90 ml pastry cream
- 540 ml chicken broth-3 cups
- 1/2 tsp paprika spice seasoning
- 1/2 tsp thyme
- 1/2 tsp red pepper flakes
- salt
- pepper

DIRECTIONS:

1. Set the air fryer to grill and preheat to 200° C. Cut the peppers in half and core them.
2. Then moisten with olive oil inside and outside.
3. Put the peppers on the baking tray (use parchment paper) and grill for 10-15 minutes.
4. While the peppers are cooking, cut the cauliflower into florets.
5. Remove the ready-grilled peppers from the air fryer and place in zip-closed freezer bags or a container with a lid. Now place the cauliflower florets on the baking sheet.
6. Mix 1 tbsp olive oil with salt and pepper. Use it to coat the cauliflower.
7. Put the plate in the air fryer and cook the cauliflower for 30 to 35 minutes at 200° C with circulating air (do not forget to switch from "grilling" to "convection").
8. Remove the skin from the peppers.
9. Dice the spring onions. Heat 2 tablespoon of olive oil in the pot and sauté the onions.

10. Once the spring onions are seared, add the spices. Mix everything well and let the spices release their aroma.
11. Now add the peppers. Let them fry for a moment. Then add the chicken broth, red pepper, and cauliflower.
12. Simmer for another 10-20 minutes at low temperature.
13. .Pour the pastry cream into it. Take the soup from the hob and purée with a blender for about 2 minutes.
14. Season to taste. Before serving, dice the feta cheese, spread on top and garnish with thyme and spring onions.

NUTRITION: Calories: 68 Fat: 4g Carbs: 8g Protein: 1g

169. Low-carb Tomato Soup

Preparation Time: 10 minutes
Cooking Time:
Servings: 4
INGREDIENTS:
- 800 g tomatoes
- 20 g butter
- 1/4 onion (red onion)
- 1 clove of garlic
- 250 ml vegetable broth
- 4 tsp olive oil
- 8 g erythritol
- 1 pinch of salt
- 1 pinch of pepper

DIRECTIONS:
1. Carefully slice into the tomatoes in a crosswise pattern
2. Put the tomatoes briefly in boiling water and then quench with cold water
3. Skin tomatoes with a knife and chop tomatoes
4. Chop onions, garlic, and basil
5. Sauté with butter
6. Broth to give and boil briefly
7. Add the tomatoes and simmer for 10 minutes
8. Transfer to a blender and puree

NUTRITION: Calories: 159 Fat: 10g Carbs: 7g Protein: 4g

170. Pea Soup with Roasted Asparagus & Feta

Preparation Time: 10 minutes
Cooking Time: 20 minutes
Servings: 4
INGREDIENTS:
- 500 g frozen peas
- 100 g green asparagus
- 200 g feta
- 2 shallots
- 4 spring onions
- 100 g potatoes, floury
- 800 ml vegetable broth
- Ginger, freshly grated
- 3 tbsp olive oil
- 1/2 bunch of basil
- nutmeg
- sea salt
- pepper

DIRECTIONS:
1. Peel the shallots and finely chop them
2. Wash spring onions and cut into rings
3. Peel and cut the potatoes Peel the asparagus in the lower third, then cut the bars into 3 cm long piece
4. Wash the basil and shake dry, four beautiful stems for the garnish set aside, chop the rest.
5. Heat 2 tbsp of oil in a frying air fryer and sauté potatoes with shallots and spring onions. Deglaze everything with the stock and then simmer for about 10 minutes. Add frozen peas, bring to a simmer and simmer for another 5 minutes.
6. Add the ginger and basil to the soup
7. Remove the pot from the stove and finely puree everything with the hand blender Season the soup with freshly grated nutmeg, salt and pepper and set aside, set aside.
8. Season the asparagus with salt and pepper Fill the soup with four bowls and add the asparagus pieces
9. Crumble the feta and add to the soup. Garnish with basil.

NUTRITION: Calories: 143 Fat: 5g Carbs: 16g Protein: 9g

171. Zucchini Soup

Preparation Time: 10 minutes
Cooking Time: 15 – 20 minutes
Servings: 4
INGREDIENTS:

- 400 g zucchini
- 1 onion
- 1 clove of garlic
- 50 g potatoes
- 2 sprigs of thyme
- 1 sprig rosemary
- 500 ml vegetable stock
- 100 ml cream
- 4 tbsp olive oil
- 1 tbsp butter
- nutmeg
- sea salt
- pepper

DIRECTIONS:

1. Rinse and dry the zucchini, then cut into quarters and cut into pieces of about 1 cm. Peel the onion, garlic and finely dice. Peel and grate the potatoes.
2. Wash the thyme and rosemary, shake dry and pluck the leaves from the stem. Finely chop the herbs.
3. Heat the butter and 2 ml of oil in an air fryer and sauté the onion and garlic. Add the potato and steam briefly.
4. Deglaze with the stock and simmer the vegetables for about 10 minutes with the pot closed. Add the zucchini and cook for another 5 minutes.
5. Remove the air fryer and add the cream.
6. Puree everything with a hand blender Season the soup with freshly grated nutmeg, salt, and pepper.
7. Arrange the soup in small bowls, drizzle with a spoonful of oil and garnish with fresh herbs.

NUTRITION: Calories: 70 Fat: 3g Carbs: 11g Protein: 2g

172. Tomato Soup with Cream Cheese & Parsley

Preparation Time: 10 minutes

Cooking Time: 30 minutes
Servings: 4
INGREDIENTS:

- 1 kg ripe tomatoes
- 200 ml vegetable broth
- 1 pepper
- 3 cloves of garlic
- 2 onions
- 1 chili pepper
- Juice of a lemon, organic
- 5-6 stems of basil
- 4 tbsp olive oil
- 1 tsp honey
- 100 g cream cheese
- 1/2 bunch of thyme
- 1/2 bunch of parsley
- sea salt
- pepper

DIRECTIONS:

1. Wash and drain the tomatoes, and herbs Halve the chili pepper, remove the kernels and chop finely. Pick the basil leaves off the stalk Peel and finely chop the onions and garlic Wash the peppers, cut in half, remove the seeds and partitions, and cut into pieces.
2. Heat 1 tablespoon of oil in an air fryer and roast the onions, garlic, and basil leaves Add the tomatoes to a large casserole dish and add onions, garlic, and basil.
3. Put the thyme sprigs, and a little oil over the tomatoes Bake the tomatoes in the casserole dish in a preheated air fryer at 170° C for about 30 minutes. Remove the thyme sprigs after baking. Remove the skin on fresh tomatoes after the baking time.
4. Get 2 tbsp of olive oil in the large pot and sauté paprika, chili, tomatoes, onions, garlic, and basil. Remove the pot from the heat and finely puree with the hand blender.
5. Put the pot with the tomato puree back on the hotplate and top up with the stock. Cover everything for about 20 minutes. If necessary, add a little water.
6. Add the lemon juice and honey to the tomato soup and stir Season the soup with salt and pepper.

7. Chop the parsley Put the tomato soup in deep plates or bowls and stir in a little cream cheese Sprinkle with parsley and serve.

NUTRITION: Calories: 127 Fat: 6g Carbs: 12g Protein: 6g

173. Pumpkin Soup with Roasted Cashews

Preparation Time: 10 minutes
Cooking Time: 20 minutes
Servings: 4
INGREDIENTS:

- 1/2 Hokkaido pumpkin
- 2 carrots
- 1 shallot
- 3 cm ginger
- 1/2 chili pepper
- 40 g butter
- 750 ml vegetable broth
- 100 ml orange juice, juice
- 1 tbsp of lemon juice, freshly squeezed
- 4 tbsp pumpkin seed oil
- 4 tbsp of cashew nuts
- 3-4 stems of parsley
- 4 flowers nasturtium
- sea salt
- White pepper

DIRECTIONS:

1. Thoroughly wash the pumpkin with warm water, then dry. Cut the pumpkin in half with a large knife and remove the seeds with a spoon. Cut a pumpkin half into small pieces.
2. Peel and slice the carrots Peel the shallot and finely dice it Peel the ginger, chop it into small pieces Halve the chili, core it, and cut it into pieces.
3. Melt the butter in an air fryer and sauté the shallot Add the carrots and the pumpkin and sauté everything Deglaze with the stock and pour in Add the chili pepper and simmer for 15 minutes over medium heat.
4. Meanwhile, wash the parsley, shake dry and chop Roast cashews in an air fryer without fat on all sides Then place cashews on a kitchen board and chop with a large knife.

5. Stir in the ginger, lemon and orange juice and then remove the pot from the hot plate. Puree the soup with the hand blender. Add some warm water to the soup if necessary and mix until it has the desired consistency.
6. Season the pumpkin soup with salt and pepper Fill the soup with small bowls and drizzle with pumpkin seed oil Add the parsley and cashews to the soup garnish with the edible flower.

NUTRITION: Calories: 193 Fat: 10g Carbs: 21g Protein: 5g

174. Vegetable Soup

Preparation Time: 10 minutes
Cooking Time: 35 minutes
Servings: 4
INGREDIENTS:

- 2 ml olive oil
- 1 stalk onion
- 3 tbsp chili powder
- 1 stalk carrot
- 2 stalk potatoes
- 300 g tomatoes
- 1 l vegetable soup
- 1 can Kidney beans
- 130 G peas
- 1 can Corn
- 70 G fresh cream Cheese
- 1 pinch salt
- 1 pinch pepper
- 1 shot Salsa

DIRECTIONS:

1. Heat oil in an air fryer and sauté the chopped onions. Then add the chili powder and mix well.
2. Then fry the chopped carrot, the diced potatoes, and the sliced tomatoes for 2-3 minutes. Add the vegetables to the soup and cook on medium with a lid for 20 minutes.
3. Finally add the corn, peas and beans and cook the soup for another 10 minutes.
4. To thicken the soup, add the fresh cream and season with salt, pepper, and salsa.

NUTRITION: Calories: 156 Fat: 2g Carbs: 29g Protein: 5g

DIABETICS AIR FRYER DESSERTS

175. Cheesecake Bites

Preparation Time: 40 minutes
Cooking Time: 9 minutes
Servings: 4
INGREDIENTS:

- 1/2 cup almond flour
- 2 tablespoons erythritol sweeteners plus 1/2 cup, divided
- 8 ounces cream cheese, reduced fat, softened
- 1/2 teaspoon vanilla extract, unsweetened
- 4 tablespoons heavy cream, reduced fat, divided

DIRECTIONS:

1. Prepare the cheesecake mixture, and for this, place softened cream cheese in a bowl, add cream, vanilla, and 1/2 cup sweetener and whisk using an electric mixer until smooth.
2. Scoop the mixture on a baking sheet lined with parchment sheet, then place it in the freezer for 30 minutes until firm.
3. Place flour in a small bowl and stir in the remaining sweetener.
4. Then switch on the air fryer, insert the fryer basket, grease it with olive oil, then shut with its lid, set the fryer at 350 degrees F, and preheat for 5 minutes.
5. Meanwhile, cut the cheesecake mix into bite-size pieces and then coat it with an almond flour mixture.
6. Open the fryer, add cheesecake bites in it, close with its lid, and cook for 2 minutes until nicely golden and crispy.
7. Serve straight away.

NUTRITION: Calories: 198 Carbs: 6 g Fat: 18 g Protein: 3 g

176. Coconut Pie

Preparation Time: 5 minutes
Cooking Time: 45 minutes
Servings: 6
INGREDIENTS:

- 1/2 cup coconut flour
- 1/2 cup erythritol sweetener
- 1 cup shredded coconut, unsweetened, divided
- 1/4 cup butter, unsalted
- 1 1/2 teaspoon vanilla extract, unsweetened
- 2 eggs, pastured
- 1 1/2 cups milk, low-fat, unsweetened
- 1/4 cup shredded coconut, toasted

DIRECTIONS:

1. Switch on the air fryer, insert fryer basket, grease it with olive oil, then shut with its lid, set the fryer at 350 degrees F, and preheat for 5 minutes.
2. Meanwhile, place all the ingredients in a bowl and whisk until well blended and smooth batter comes together.
3. Take a 6-inches pie pan, grease it oil, then pour in the prepared batter and smooth the top.
4. Open the fryer, place the pie pan in it, close with its lid, and cook for 45 minutes until pie has set and inserted a toothpick into the pie slide out clean.
5. When the air fryer beeps, open its lid, take out the pie pan and let it cool.
6. Garnish the pie with toasted coconut then cut into slices and serve.

NUTRITION: Calories: 236 Carbs: 16 g Fat: 16 g Protein: 3 g

177. Crustless Cheesecake

Preparation Time: 5 minutes
Cooking Time: 10 minutes
Servings: 2
INGREDIENTS:

- 16 ounces cream cheese, reduced fat, softened
- 2 tablespoons sour cream, reduced fat
- 3/4 cup erythritol sweetener
- 1 teaspoon vanilla extract, unsweetened
- 2 eggs, pastured

- 1/2 teaspoon lemon juice

DIRECTIONS:

1. Switch on the air fryer, insert fryer basket, grease it with olive oil, then shut with its lid, set the fryer at 350 degrees F, and preheat for 5 minutes.
2. Meanwhile, take two 4 inches of springform pans, grease them with oil, and set them aside.
3. Crack the eggs in a bowl and then whisk in lemon juice, sweetener, and vanilla until smooth.
4. Whisk in cream cheese and sour cream until blended, divide the mixture evenly between prepared pans.
5. Open the fryer, place pans in it, close with its lid, and cook for 10 minutes until cakes are set and inserted skewer into the cakes slide out clean.
6. When air fryer beeps, open its lid, take out the cake pans and let cakes cool in them.
7. Take out the cakes, refrigerate for 3 hours until cooled, and then serve.

NUTRITION: Calories: 318 Carbs: 1 g Fat: 29.7 g Protein: 11.7 g

178. Chocolate Cake

Preparation Time: 5 minutes
Cooking Time: 15 minutes
Servings: 6
INGREDIENTS:

- 1/4 cup coconut flour
- 1 teaspoon baking powder
- 1/3 cup Truvia sweetener
- 1/4 teaspoon salt
- 2 tablespoon cocoa powder, unsweetened
- 1 teaspoon vanilla extract, unsweetened
- 4 tablespoons butter, unsalted, melted
- 3 eggs, pastured
- 1/2 cup heavy whipping cream, reduced fat

Directions:

1. Switch on the air fryer, insert fryer basket, grease it with olive oil, then shut with its lid, set the fryer at 350 degrees F, and preheat for 5 minutes.
2. Meanwhile, take a 6 cups muffin pan, grease it with oil, and set aside until required.

3. Place melted butter in a bowl, whisk in sweetener until blended, and then beat in vanilla, eggs, and cream until combined.
4. Add remaining ingredients, beat again until incorporated and smooth batter comes together, and then pour the mixture into the prepared pan.
5. Open the fryer, place the pan in it, close with its lid, and cook for 10 minutes until the cake is done and inserted skewer into the cake slides out clean.
6. When air fryer beeps, open its lid, take out the cake pan and let the cake cool in it.
7. Take out the cakes, cut them into pieces, and serve.

NUTRITION: Calories: 192 Carbs: 8 g Fat: 16 g Protein: 4 g

179. Chocolate Brownies

Preparation Time: 10 minutes
Cooking Time: 45 minutes
Servings: 4
INGREDIENTS:

- 1/2 cup chocolate chips, sugar-free
- 1 teaspoon vanilla extract, unsweetened
- 1/4 cup erythritol sweetener
- 1/2 cup butter, unsalted
- 3 eggs, pastured

DIRECTIONS:

1. Switch on the air fryer, insert fryer basket, grease it with olive oil, then shut with its lid, set the fryer at 350 degrees F, and preheat for 10 minutes.
2. Add butter and chocolate in a microwaveable bowl and set for 1 minute or until chocolate has melted, stirring every 30 seconds.
3. Crack eggs in another bowl, beat in vanilla and sweetener until smooth and then slowly beat in melted chocolate mixture until well incorporated.
4. Take a springform pan that fits into the air fryer, grease it with oil and then pour in batter in it.
5. Open the fryer, place the pan in it, close with its lid and cook for 35 minutes until cake is done and inserted toothpick into the brownies slide out clean.

6. When air fryer beeps, open its lid, take out the pan and let the brownies cool in it.
7. Then take out the brownies, cut it into even pieces, and serve.

NUTRITION: Calories: 224 Carbs: 3 g Fat: 23 g Protein: 4 g

180. Spiced Apples

Preparation Time: 5 minutes
Cooking Time: 17 minutes
Servings: 4
INGREDIENTS:

- 4 small apples, cored, sliced
- 2 tablespoons erythritol sweeteners
- 1 teaspoon apple pie spice
- 2 tablespoons olive oil

DIRECTIONS:

1. Switch on the air fryer, insert fryer basket, grease it with olive oil, then shut with its lid, set the fryer at 350 degrees F, and preheat for 5 minutes.
2. Meanwhile, place apple slices in a bowl, sprinkle with sweetener and spice, and drizzle with oil and stir until evenly coated.
3. Open the fryer, add apple slices in it, close with its lid and cook for 12 minutes until nicely golden and crispy, shaking halfway through the frying.
4. Serve straight away.

NUTRITION: Calories: 89.6 Carbs: 21.8 g Fat: 2 g Protein: 0.5 g

181. Chocolate Lava Cake

Preparation Time: 5 minutes
Cooking Time: 13 minutes
Servings: 2
INGREDIENTS:

- 1 tablespoon flax meal
- 1/2 teaspoon baking powder
- 2 tablespoons cocoa powder, unsweetened
- 2 tablespoons erythritol sweeteners
- 1/8 teaspoon Stevia sweetener
- 1/8 teaspoon vanilla extract, unsweetened
- 1 tablespoon olive oil
- 2 tablespoons water
- 1 egg, pastured

DIRECTIONS:

1. Switch on the air fryer, insert fryer basket, grease it with olive oil, then shut with its lid, set the fryer at 350 degrees F, and preheat for 5 minutes.
2. Meanwhile, take a two cups ramekin, grease it with oil and set aside.
3. Get a small bowl and put all ingredients. Mix until well combined and incorporated. Pour the batter into the ramekin.
4. Open the fryer, place ramekin in it, close with its lid and cook for 8 minutes until cake is done and inserted skewer into the cake slides out clean.
5. When air fryer beeps, open its lid, take out the ramekin and let the cake cool in it.
6. Then take out the cake, cut it into slices, and serve.

NUTRITION: Calories: 362.8 Carbs: 3.4 g Fat: 33.6 g Protein: 11.7 g

182. Pecan Pie Bread Pudding

Preparation Time: 10 minutes
Cooking Time: 15 minutes
Servings: 4
INGREDIENTS:

- 2 cups (1") cubes gluten-free sandwich bread
- 1/2 cup pecan pieces
- 3 large eggs
- 1/4 cup half-and-half
- 1/4 cup dark corn syrup
- 1 teaspoon vanilla extract
- 2 tablespoons dark brown sugar
- 1/4 teaspoon ground cinnamon
- 1/4 teaspoon salt

DIRECTIONS:

1. Place bread pieces in an ungreased 7" square cake barrel and spread pecan pieces evenly over the top.
2. In a medium bowl, whisk eggs. Stir in remaining ingredients.
3. Pour egg mixture over bread and pecans in cake barrel. Let sit 10 minutes.
4. Preheat air fryer at 325°F for 3 minutes.
5. Place cake pan in the air fryer basket. Cook 15 minutes.

6. Transfer the pan to a cooling rack for 10 minutes. Once cooled slightly, slice and serve warm.

NUTRITION: Calories: 290 Fat: 25g Carbs: 16g Protein: 3g

183. Pumpkin Crunch Cake

Preparation Time: 15 minutes
Cooking Time: 35 minutes
Servings: 6
INGREDIENTS:
- For Crunch Layer
- 1/3 cup pecan pieces
- 5 gluten-free gingersnap cookies
- 1/3 cup light brown sugar
- 3 tablespoons butter, melted
- For Cake
- 3 large eggs
- 3 tablespoons butter, melted
- 1/2 teaspoon vanilla extract
- 1 cup pumpkin purée
- 2 tablespoons sour cream
- 1/2 cup gluten-free all-purpose flour
- 1/4 cup tapioca flour
- 1/2 teaspoon xanthan gum
- 1/2 cup granulated sugar
- 1/2 teaspoon baking soda
- 1 teaspoon baking powder
- 1 teaspoon pumpkin pie spice
- 1/8 teaspoon salt
- For Cream Cheese Frosting
- 6 ounces cream cheese, room temperature
- 11/3 cups powdered sugar
- 1/2 teaspoon vanilla extract
- 2 tablespoons butter, room temperature
- 1 tablespoon whole milk

DIRECTIONS:
1. Place parchment paper in a pan. Put preferred cooking oil in paper and sides of pan lightly.
2. To make Crunch Layer: In a food processor, pulse Crunch Layer ingredients until combined. Press mixture into the bottom of the cake pan.
3. To make Cake: Whisk together wet cake ingredients in a medium bowl. In a large bowl, sift together dry cake ingredients.
4. Warm air fryer at 350°F for 3 minutes.
5. Put wet ingredients to dry ingredients and gently combine. Do not overmix. Pour mixture into a cake pan. Cover with aluminum foil.
6. Place cake pan in the air fryer basket. Cook 30 minutes. Remove foil. Cook an additional 5 minutes.
7. Transfer cake pan to a cooling rack to cool 10 minutes. Once cooled, flip the cake onto a large serving platter.
8. To make Cream Cheese Frosting: Cream together frosting ingredients in a small bowl. Spread over cooled cake. Slice and serve.

NUTRITION: Calories: 253 Fat: 14g Carbs: 29g Protein: 4g

184. Carrot Cake Cupcakes

Preparation Time: 10 minutes
Cooking Time: 14 minutes
Servings: 8
INGREDIENTS:
- For Cupcakes
- 1 cup gluten-free all-purpose flour
- 1/2 teaspoon baking soda
- 1/3 cup light brown sugar
- 1/4 teaspoon salt
- 1/4 teaspoon ground cinnamon
- 1/8 teaspoon ground ginger
- 1 teaspoon vanilla extract
- 1 large egg
- 1 tablespoon buttermilk
- 1 tablespoon vegetable oil
- 1/4 cup grated carrots
- 2 tablespoons coconut shreds
- For Cream Cheese Frosting
- 6 ounces cream cheese, room temperature
- 11/3 cups powdered sugar
- 1/2 teaspoon vanilla extract
- 2 tablespoons butter, room temperature
- 1 tablespoon whole milk
- 1/2 cup chopped walnuts

DIRECTIONS:

1. To make Cupcakes: In a large bowl, combine flour, baking soda, sugar, salt, cinnamon, ginger, and vanilla. In a medium bowl, combine egg, buttermilk, oil, carrots, and coconut.
2. Preheat air fryer at 375°F for 3 minutes.
3. Pour wet ingredients from a medium bowl into a large bowl with dry ingredients. Gently combine. Do not overmix. Spoon mixture into eight silicone cupcake liners lightly greased with preferred cooking oil.
4. Place four cupcake liners in an air fryer basket. Cook 7 minutes.
5. Transfer cooked cupcakes to a cooling rack and let sit for 15 minutes. Repeat with remaining cupcakes.
6. To make Cream Cheese Frosting: In a small bowl, beat cream cheese, sugar, vanilla, butter, and milk until smooth.
7. Spread frosting on cooled cupcakes. Sprinkle tops with chopped walnuts. Serve.

NUTRITION: Calories: 143 Fat: 1.9g Carbs: 24g Protein: 6g

185. Apple Crumble Jars

Preparation Time: 15 minutes
Cooking Time: 24 minutes
Servings: 6
INGREDIENTS:
- For Apple Filling
- 3 cups diced, peeled, seeded Granny Smith apples (approximately 3 large)
- tablespoon lemon juice
- 1 tablespoon gluten-free all-purpose flour
- 2 tablespoons light brown sugar
- 1/2 teaspoon ground cinnamon
- 1 tablespoon butter, melted
- 1/8 teaspoon salt
- 6 (4-ounce) glass jelly jars
- For Crumble Topping
- 2 tablespoons gluten-free all-purpose flour
- 1/3 cup old-fashioned oats
- 1/4 cup chopped pecans
- 4 teaspoons light brown sugar
- 1/4 teaspoon ground cinnamon
- 1/8 teaspoon ground nutmeg
- 2 tablespoons butter, melted

- 1/8 teaspoon salt

DIRECTIONS:
1. To make Apple Filling: Place diced apples in a medium bowl and toss with lemon juice. Add remaining filling ingredients and toss.
2. Ready air fryer at 350°F for 3 minutes.
3. Distribute apple mixture among jelly jars. Place three jars in the air fryer basket. Cook 7 minutes. Repeat with remaining jars.
4. To make Crumble Topping: While the apple mixture is cooking, combine Crumble Topping ingredients in a medium bowl.
5. Once the cooked put Crumble Topping. Bake for another 5 minutes in batches of three jars.
6. Let jars cool 10 minutes before covering. Refrigerate until ready to serve, up to 4 days.

NUTRITION: Calories: 250 Fat: 8g Carbs: 29g Protein: 3g

186. Tortilla Sopapilla

Preparation Time: 5 minutes
Cooking Time: 4 minutes
Servings: 8
INGREDIENTS:
- 2 tablespoons granulated sugar
- 1/2 teaspoon ground cinnamon
- 1/8 teaspoon salt
- 8 (6") gluten-free flour tortillas, quartered
- 2 tablespoons butter, melted
- 4 teaspoons honey
- tablespoon powdered sugar

DIRECTIONS:
1. Preheat air fryer to 400°F for 5 minutes.
2. In a small bowl, mix well the sugar, cinnamon, and salt. Set aside.
3. Brush tortilla quarters with melted butter. Sprinkle sugar mixture over brushed tortillas.
4. Add prepared tortillas to an ungreased air fryer basket. Cook 2 minutes. Toss tortillas, then cook an additional 2 minutes.
5. Transfer sopapillas to a large plate. Let cool 5 minutes to allow to harden.

6. Drizzle hardened sopapillas with honey and sprinkled with powdered sugar. Serve.

NUTRITION: Calories: 114 Fat: 1g Carbs: 22g Protein: 2g

187. Kiwi Pavlova with Lemon Cream

Preparation Time: 15 minutes
Cooking Time: 90 minutes
Servings: 2
INGREDIENTS:

- For Pavlova
- 2 egg whites
- 1/4 teaspoon cornstarch
- 1/2 cup granulated sugar
- 1/2 teaspoon lemon juice
- 1/2 teaspoon vanilla extract
- For Topping
- 1/3 cup heavy whipping cream
- 1 teaspoon lemon juice
- 1/4 teaspoon lemon zest
- 2 tablespoons granulated sugar
- 2 medium kiwis, peeled and sliced

DIRECTIONS:

1. To make Pavlova:
2. Get a grill pan and cut a piece of parchment to the size of it. Make a circle (6 inches) on paper.
3. Turn the paper onto grill pan. You have to see circle outline. Set aside.
4. Get a large metal bowl. Prepare an electric mixer, set to high speed, and beat egg whites.
5. Add cornstarch while beating. Put 1 tbsp. of sugar at a time, until stiff peaks form in the mixture. Add lemon juice and vanilla.
6. Prepare the air fryer at 225°F for 5 minutes.
7. Put egg white mixture over parchment paper circle, creating higher edges around perimeter (like a short pie crust). Make an indention in center.
8. Arrange grill pan to fryer basket and cook 60 minutes.
9. Once cooked. Turn off heat and leave for 30 minutes.

10. Take the grill pan and slowly peel off parchment paper from bottom of pavlova. Move the pavlova to a plate.
11. To make Topping:
12. Get a medium bowl, whisk together whipping cream, lemon juice, lemon zest, and sugar until creamy.
13. Fill pavlova crust with whipped cream mixture and top with kiwi slices. Serve.

NUTRITION: Calories: 320 Fat: 13g Carbs: 40g Protein: 4g

188. Amaretto Cheesecake

Preparation Time: 10 minutes
Cooking Time: 22 minutes
Servings: 6
INGREDIENTS:

- For Crust
- 1/2 cup Corn Chex
- 2/3 cup blanched slivered almonds
- 1 tablespoon light brown sugar
- 3 tablespoons butter, melted
- For Cheesecake
- 14 ounces cream cheese, room temperature
- 2 tablespoons sour cream
- 1 large egg
- 1/2 cup granulated sugar
- 1/2 cup Amaretto liqueur
- 1/2 teaspoon lemon juice
- 1/8 teaspoon salt

DIRECTIONS:

1. To make Crust: Pulse Corn Chex, almonds, and brown sugar in a food processor until it has a powdered consistency.
2. Put into a small bowl and add melted butter. Combine with a fork until butter is well distributed. Press mixture into a 7" springform pan lightly greased with preferred cooking oil.
3. Preheat air fryer at 400°F for 3 minutes.
4. To make Cheesecake: Combine cream cheese, sour cream, egg, sugar, Amaretto, lemon juice, and salt in a large bowl. Spoon over crust. Cover with aluminum foil.
5. Place springform pan in air fryer basket and cook 16 minutes. Remove aluminum foil and cook an additional 6 minutes.

6. Remove cheesecake from air fryer basket. Cheesecake will be a little jiggly in center.
7. Cover and refrigerate at least 2 hours to allow it to set. Once set, release side pan, and serve.

NUTRITION: Calories: 280 Fat: 14g Carbs: 29g Protein: 4g

189. Lemon Cheesecake with Raspberry Sauce

Preparation Time: 10 minutes
Cooking Time: 22 minutes
Servings: 6
INGREDIENTS:

- For Crust
- 1 cup cornflakes cereal
- 2 tablespoons granulated sugar
- 4 tablespoons butter, melted
- For Cheesecake
- 12 ounces cream cheese, room temperature
- 2 tablespoons sour cream
- 2 large eggs
- 1/2 cup granulated sugar
- 1 tablespoon lemon zest
- 1 tablespoon fresh lemon juice
- 1 teaspoon vanilla extract
- 1/8 teaspoon salt
- For Raspberry Sauce
- 1 1/2 cups fresh raspberries
- 2 tablespoons lemon juice
- 1/2 cup granulated sugar

DIRECTIONS:

1. To make Crust: Pulse together cornflakes, sugar, and butter in a food processor. Press mixture into a 7" springform pan lightly greased with preferred cooking oil.
2. Preheat air fryer at 400°F for 3 minutes.
3. To make Cheesecake: Combine cream cheese, sour cream, eggs, sugar, lemon zest, lemon juice, vanilla, and salt in a large bowl. Spoon into crust. Cover with aluminum foil.
4. Place springform pan in air fryer basket and cook 16 minutes. Remove aluminum foil and cook an additional 6 minutes.
5. To make Raspberry Sauce: While cheesecake is baking, add Raspberry Sauce

ingredients to a small saucepan over medium heat and cook 5 minutes. Using back of spoon, smoosh raspberries against side of saucepan while cooking. After berries are smooshed and sauce has thickened, pour through a sieve to filter out seeds. Refrigerate covered until ready to use.
6. Remove cheesecake from air fryer. Cheesecake will be a little jiggly in center. Cover and refrigerate at least 2 hours to allow it to set. Once set, release side pan, and serve with Raspberry Sauce poured over slices.

NUTRITION: Calories: 268 Fat: 8g Carbs: 35g Protein: 12g

190. Perfect Cinnamon Toast

Preparation Time: 5 minutes
Cooking Time: 5 – 10 minutes
Servings: 1
INGREDIENTS:

- 2 tsp. pepper
- 1 1/2 tsp. vanilla extract
- 1 1/2 tsp. cinnamon
- 1/2 C. sweetener of choice
- 1 C. coconut oil
- 12 slices whole-wheat bread

DIRECTIONS:

1. Melt coconut oil and mix with sweetener until dissolved. Mix in remaining ingredients minus bread till incorporated.
2. Spread mixture onto bread, covering all areas. Place coated pieces of bread in your air fryer.
3. Cook 5 minutes at 400 degrees F.
4. Remove and cut diagonally. Enjoy!

NUTRITION: Calories: 124 Fat: 2g Protein: 2g Sugar: 17g

191. Apple Dumplings

Preparation Time: 10 minutes
Cooking Time: 25 minutes
Servings: 4
INGREDIENTS:

- 2 tbsp. melted coconut oil
- 2 puff pastry sheets

- 1 tbsp. brown sugar
- 2 tbsp. raisins
- 2 small apples of choice

DIRECTIONS:
1. Ensure your air fryer is preheated to 356 degrees F.
2. Core and peel apples and mix with raisins and sugar.
3. Place a bit of apple mixture into puff pastry sheets and brush sides with melted coconut oil.
4. Place into air fryer. Cook 25 minutes, turning halfway through. It will be golden when done.

NUTRITION: Calories: 260 Fat: 7g Protein: 2g Carbs: 35g

192. Easy Air Fryer Donuts

Preparation Time: 10 minutes
Cooking Time: 10 – 15 minutes
Servings: 8
INGREDIENTS:
- Pinch of allspice
- 4 tbsp. dark brown sugar
- 1/2 - 1 tsp. cinnamon
- 1/3 C. granulated sweetener
- 3 tbsp. melted coconut oil
- 1 can of biscuits

DIRECTIONS:
1. Mix allspice, sugar, sweetener, and cinnamon.
2. Take out biscuits from the can and with a circle cookie cutter, cut holes from centers, and place into the air fryer.
3. Cook 5 minutes at 350 degrees F. As batches are cooked, use a brush to coat with melted coconut oil and dip each into a sugar mixture.
4. Serve warm!

NUTRITION: Calories: 209 Fat: 4g Protein: 5g Carbs: 39g

193. Chocolate Soufflé for Two

Preparation Time: 10 minutes
Cooking Time: 15 minutes
Servings: 2

INGREDIENTS:
- 2 tbsp. almond flour
- 1/2 tsp. vanilla
- 3 tbsp. sweetener
- 2 separated eggs
- 1/4 C. melted coconut oil
- 3 ounces of semi-sweet chocolate, chopped

DIRECTIONS:
1. Brush coconut oil and sweetener onto ramekins.
2. Melt coconut oil and chocolate together.
3. Beat egg yolks well, adding vanilla and sweetener. Stir in flour and ensure there are no lumps.
4. Preheat fryer to 330 degrees .
5. Whisk egg whites till they reach peak state and fold them into chocolate mixture.
6. Pour batter into ramekins and place into the fryer.
7. Cook 14 minutes.
8. Serve with powdered sugar dusted on top.

NUTRITION: Calories: 238 Fat: 6g Protein: 1g Carbs: 23g

194. Apple Hand Pies

Preparation Time: 10 minutes
Cooking Time: 10 minutes
Servings: 6
Ingredients:
- 15-ounces no-sugar-added apple pie filling
- 1 store-bought crust

DIRECTIONS:
1. Layout pie crust and slice into equal-sized squares.
2. Place 2 tbsp. Filling into each square and seal crust with a fork.
3. Place into the fryer. Cook 8 minutes at 390 degrees until golden in color.

NUTRITION: Calories: 278 Fat: 10g Protein: 5g Carbs: 23g

195. Blueberry Lemon Muffins

Preparation Time: 10 minutes
Cooking Time: 10 minutes
Servings: 12
INGREDIENTS:
- 1 tsp. vanilla

- Juice and zest of 1 lemon
- 2 eggs
- 1 C. blueberries
- 1/2 C. cream
- 1/4 C. avocado oil
- 1/2 C. monk fruit
- 2 1/2 C. almond flour

DIRECTIONS:
1. Mix monk fruit and flour.
2. In another bowl, mix vanilla, egg, lemon juice, and cream.
3. Add mixtures together and blend well.
4. Spoon batter into cupcake holders. Place in an air fryer. Bake 10 minutes at 320 degrees F, checking at 6 minutes to ensure you don't overbake them.

NUTRITION: Calories: 317 Fat: 11g Protein: 3g Carbs: 31g

196. Sweet Cream Cheese Wontons

Preparation Time: 10 minutes
Cooking Time: 10 minutes
Servings: 16
INGREDIENTS:
- 1 egg mixed with a bit of water
- Wonton wrappers
- 1/2 C. powdered erythritol
- 8 ounces softened cream cheese
- Olive oil

DIRECTIONS:
1. Mix sweetener and cream cheese together.
2. Layout 4 wontons at a time and cover with a dish towel to prevent drying out.
3. Place 1/2 of a teaspoon of cream cheese mixture into each wrapper.
4. Dip finger into egg/water mixture and fold diagonally to form a triangle. Seal edges well.
5. Repeat with remaining ingredients.
6. Place filled wontons into the air fryer and cook 5 minutes at 400 degrees F, shaking halfway through cooking.

NUTRITION: Calories: 188 Fat: 3g Protein: 4g Carbs: 27g

197. Cinnamon Rolls

Preparation Time: 1 hour
Cooking Time: 15 minutes
Servings: 8
INGREDIENTS:
- 1 1/2 tbsp. cinnamon
- 3/4 C. brown sugar
- 1/4 C. melted coconut oil
- 1-pound frozen bread dough, thawed
- Glaze:
- 1/2 tsp. vanilla
- 1 1/4 C. powdered erythritol
- 2 tbsp. softened ghee
- 4 ounces softened cream cheese

DIRECTIONS:
1. Layout bread dough and roll it out into a rectangle. Brush melted ghee over the dough and leave a 1-inch border along the edges.
2. Mix cinnamon and sweetener and then sprinkle over dough.
3. Roll dough tightly and slice into 8 pieces. Let sit 1-2 hours to rise.
4. To make the glaze, mix ingredients till smooth.
5. Once rolls rise, place into the air fryer and cook 5 minutes at 350 degrees F.
6. Serve rolls drizzled in cream cheese glaze. Enjoy!

NUTRITION: Calories: 234 Fat: 7g Protein: 3g Carbs: 39g

198. French Toast Bites

Preparation Time: 5 minutes
Cooking Time: 15 minutes
Servings: 8
INGREDIENTS:
- Almond milk
- Cinnamon
- Sweetener
- 3 eggs
- 4 pieces wheat bread

DIRECTIONS:
1. Preheat air fryer to 360 degrees F.
2. Whisk eggs and thin out with almond milk.

3. Mix 1/3 cup of sweetener with lots of cinnamon.
4. Tear bread in half, ball up pieces and press together to form a ball.
5. Soak bread balls in egg and then roll into cinnamon sugar, making sure to coat thoroughly.
6. Place coated bread balls into air fryer and bake 15 minutes.

NUTRITION: Calories: 289 Fat: 11g Protein: 5g Carbs: 45g

199. Baked Apple

Preparation Time: 10 minutes
Cooking Time: 10 minutes
Servings: 4
INGREDIENTS:
- 1/4 C. water
- 1/4 tsp. nutmeg
- 1/4 tsp. cinnamon
- 1 1/2 tsp. melted ghee
- 2 tbsp. raisins
- 2 tbsp. chopped walnuts
- 1 medium apple

DIRECTIONS:
1. Preheat your air fryer to 350 degrees.
2. Slice an apple in half and discard some of the flesh from the center.
3. Place into a frying pan.
4. Mix remaining ingredients together except water. Spoon mixture to the middle of apple halves.
5. Pour water overfilled apples.
6. Place pan with apple halves into the air fryer, bake 20 minutes.

NUTRITION: Calories: 199 Fat: 9g Protein: 1g Carbs: 17g

200. Cinnamon Sugar Roasted Chickpeas

Preparation Time: 10 minutes
Cooking Time: 10 minutes
Servings: 2
INGREDIENTS:
- 1 tbsp. sweetener
- 1 tbsp. cinnamon
- 1 C. chickpeas

DIRECTIONS:
1. Preheat the air fryer to 390 degrees F.
2. Rinse and drain chickpeas.
3. Mix all ingredients and add to the air fryer.
4. Cook 10 minutes.

NUTRITION: Calories: 111 Fat: 4g Protein: 4g Carbs: 16g

201. Cinnamon Fried Bananas

Preparation Time: 10 minutes
Cooking Time: 13 minutes
Servings: 2
INGREDIENTS:
- 1 C. panko breadcrumbs
- 3 tbsp. cinnamon
- 1/2 C. almond flour
- 3 egg whites
- 8 ripe bananas
- 3 tbsp. vegan coconut oil

DIRECTIONS:
1. Heat coconut oil and add breadcrumbs. Mix around 2-3 minutes until golden. Pour into a bowl.
2. Peel and cut bananas in half. Roll the half of each banana into flour, eggs, and crumb mixture. Place into the air fryer.
3. Cook 10 minutes at 280 degrees F.
4. A great addition to a healthy banana split!

NUTRITION: Calories: 107 Fat: 0.7g Protein: 1g Carbs: 27g

30-DAY PLAN

You already heard the phrase; you are what you eat. But it is not just what you eat that affects your health, but your entire lifestyle. Everything, including your diet, exercise, medication, drinking, smoking, and sleep habits affect your health. There are other aspects of your lifestyle that can impact your health; this is only the tip of the iceberg. In this part, we will be focusing on the importance of a healthy lifestyle, both in treating and preventing chronic kidney disease.

When you have diabetes, it is incredibly important to focus on promoting healthy lifestyle factors. You can't just take some medicine and get better. Instead, you have to prioritize eating a low-protein diet with the correct proportions of nutrients, exercising to maintain healthy muscles and organs, and sleeping well so that your body has the strength to function to the best of its ability. In one study on chronic kidney disease, it was found that patients who eat a healthy diet, stay physically active, maintain healthy body weight, and don't smoke can increase their longevity greatly. The participants who met all of these healthy lifestyle qualities reduced their risks of dying from the disease by sixty-eight percent compared to those who don't follow these lifestyle choices.

This is important to consider because if your diabetes or heart health is not under control, it will put more pressure on your kidneys and increase your fatality risk. If you treat these conditions through a healthy lifestyle, you can greatly improve your diabetes or heart health and your kidney health. Overall, you can only benefit from focusing on improving your lifestyle.

Early Diagnosis:

Suppose you don't yet have chronic kidney disease, but you or a family member are at risk of developing the condition. In that case, you can reduce your risk and potentially prevent yourself from developing the disease by making healthy lifestyle changes. Remember, you are more likely to develop kidney disease if you have a family history, diabetes, heart disease, or high blood pressure. If any of these apply to you or someone you love, then consider making the beneficial lifestyle changes mentioned in this part.

To maintain a healthy body, you must maintain frequent checkups with your doctor. The frequency of these checkups will depend on your age and any preexisting conditions, and your doctor will be able to recommend a checkup schedule. For people who are in good health, a once-yearly checkup is usually enough. However, if you have any preexisting conditions such as high blood pressure and diabetes, you will need more frequent checkups.

When having your checkup, ask your doctor about monitoring your kidney health. Suppose you are concerned about having a high risk of developing this disease in the future. In that case, your doctor should easily be able to monitor your condition with just a quick urine and blood test at your regular checkups. Your doctor will also keep an eye on your blood sugar and blood pressure to check for diabetes and heart problems. Remember, early diagnosis and treatment is your best option.

If you develop a urinary tract infection, which is rather common, you need to contact your doctor immediately. The infection itself is not dangerous when treated. However, if left untreated, a urinary tract infection can cause chronic damage to your kidneys, potentially causing chronic kidney disease in the future. Thankfully, your doctor can easily prescribe you medicine to treat the infection, which should relatively quickly prevent unnecessary damage to your kidneys.

Control Your Blood Pressure:

One of the biggest steps you can take to improving your kidney health is managing your blood pressure. Most people only think about the effect blood pressure has on the heart, but it also affects other organs, such as your kidneys. You should maintain blood pressure at the goal set by your physician. Most people should aim at blood pressure less than 140/90, as anything over this is considered high.

Blood pressure can become high for different reasons. Therefore, you should discuss a plan with your doctor to lower your blood pressure. In general, lowering blood pressure can involve:

- Increased exercise
- Enough sleep
- Higher quality sleep
- Healthy meals with reduced sodium
- Quit smoking
- Taking prescribed medications

Manage Your Blood Glucose:

You need to check your blood glucose levels regularly if you have diabetes as prescribed by your doctor. You can use the results you receive to make better choices about exercise, food, and medication.

Your doctor will also test your A1C to measure your average blood glucose over the previous three months. The higher your A1C number, the higher your standard blood glucose levels were during the three months.

Maintain Low Cholesterol:

High cholesterol runs in families, and it is common in people who make poor lifestyle choices, such as eating an unhealthy diet. It is important to manage, as high cholesterol increases your heart disease and kidney disease risk. It is also possible for chronic kidney disease to increase a person's cholesterol. Thankfully, studies have shown that treating high cholesterol in patients with chronic kidney disease is the same as those without the disease. This means you can make common-sense changes to improve your cholesterol health, which will be effective even if you have been diagnosed with kidney disease.

When attempting to lower high cholesterol or maintain low cholesterol, keep in mind that there is no specific target level of cholesterol that is universal. Instead, your doctor will advise you on your specific cholesterol levels and what you should aim for.

Limit Alcohol Consumption:

By drinking too much, you can negatively raise your blood pressure and consume too many calories, which can cause weight gain and kidney damage. While there can be some benefits to drinking in moderation (unless otherwise instructed by your doctor), you should never exceed the daily recommendation. Men consume no more than one or two while women should consume no more than one drink daily. The exact amount "one drink" consists of varies depending on the type of alcohol you are drinking. One drink is either 1.5 ounces of heavy liquor, 5 ounces of wine, or 12 ounces of beer.

Day	Breakfast	Lunch	Dinner	Dessert
1	Creamy Potatoes	Crispy Fish Sandwiches	Mushrooms Marinated In Garlic Coco-aminos	Cheesecake Bites

2	Swiss Chard and Cheese Omelet	Breaded Hake With Green Chili Pepper And Mayonnaise	Potato Filled Bread Rolls	Coconut Pie
3	Ricotta and Leafy Green Omelet	Salmon With Brown Sugar Glaze	Elegant Garlic Mushroom	Crustless Cheesecake
4	Mom's Jacket Potatoes	Catfish With Green Beans	Rosemary Au Gratin Potatoes	Chocolate Cake
5	Pantano Romanesco with Goat Cheese	Honey-glazed Salmon	Three Veg Bake	Spiced Apples
6	Green Beans and Shallots	Sesame Seeds Coated Tuna	Garden Fresh Green Beans	Chocolate Brownies
7	Italian Mushroom Mix	Salmon Cakes	Tofu In Sweet & Spicy Sauce	Pecan Pie Bread Pudding
8	Oyster Mushroom and Lemongrass Omelet	Crumbed Fish	Fried Broccoli From India	Pumpkin Crunch Cake
9	Roasted Pumpkin	Shrimp With Delicious Sauce	Baked Potato Topped With Cream Cheese 'n Olives	Carrot Cake Cupcakes
10	Salmon Spring Rolls	Shrimp Scampi	Spices Stuffed Eggplants	Apple Crumble Jars
11	Herb Tomatoes	Sesame Seeds Fish Fillet	Pull-apart Bread With Garlic Oil	Tortilla Sopapilla
12	Mini Pizza	Cajun Salmon	Chickpeas & Spinach With Coconut	Kiwi Pavlova with Lemon Cream
13	Egg Rolls	Scallops With Creamy Tomato Sauce	Lemony Green Beans	Amaretto Cheesecake
14	Roasted Parsnips	Crab Cake	Creole Seasoned Vegetables	Perfect Cinnamon Toast
15	Chicken Nuggets	Saltine Wax Beans	Potato Filled Bread Rolls	Lemon Cheesecake with Raspberry Sauce
16	Spanakopita Bites	Easy Rosemary Green Beans	Low Fat Butter Chicken	Apple Dumplings
17	Kale & Celery Crackers	Sriracha Golden Cauliflower	White Chicken Chili	Easy Air Fryer Donuts
18	Roasted Corn	Cauliflower Tater Tots	Quick Paella	Cinnamon Sugar Roasted Chickpeas
19	Spinach Frittata	Chili Fingerling Potatoes	Seafood Tacos	Baked Apple
20	Vegetable Spring Rolls	Potato with Creamy Cheese	Crispy Herbed Salmon	French Toast Bites
21	Pantano Romanesco with Goat Cheese	Golden Pickles	Snapper Scampi	Cinnamon Rolls

22	Italian Mushroom Mix	Garlic Eggplant Slices	Crumbed Fish	Blueberry Lemon Muffins
23	Egg Rolls	Zucchini Balls	Sesame Seeds Fish Fillet	Cheesecake Bites
24	Salmon Spring Rolls	Lemony Falafel	Fish and Chips	Crustless Cheesecake
25	Roasted Pumpkin	Lemony and Spicy Coconut Crusted Salmon	Fried Broccoli From India	Apple Hand Pies
26	Ricotta and Leafy Green Omelet	Salmon Jerky	Potato Filled Bread Rolls	Pumpkin Crunch Cake
27	Mom's Jacket Potatoes	Hawaiian Salmon	Rosemary Au Gratin Potatoes	Coconut Pie
28	Green Beans and Shallots	Parmesan Walnut Salmon	Salmon With Brown Sugar Glaze	Sweet Cream Cheese Wontons
29	Swiss Chard and Cheese Omelet	Crispy Chickpeas	Breaded Hake With Green Chili Pepper And Mayonnaise	Cinnamon Fried Bananas
30	Oyster Mushroom and Lemongrass Omelet	Sweet and Sour Tofu	Crispy Fish Sandwiches	Chocolate Soufflé for Two

CONCLUSION

The Diabetic Air Fryer Cookbook is an essential guide for people with diabetes. Using the Air Fryer is a smart way to help your diabetes control and reduce the disease's effects.

Air frying uses less fat than conventional frying, making it a great way to reduce calories and fat in your diet. It is also an easy way to cook meals that are healthier and tasted better than ever.

This cookbook includes detailed directions on how to use the Air Fryer and has tips on storing your Air Fryer and cleaning it safely for long term use. It also contains many recipes that use this kitchen appliance to make delicious meals that are healthy, delicious, and low in calories. You learn how easy it is to prepare various delicious recipes using the Air Fryer alongside other healthy recipes created by registered dietitians and other nutrition experts.

In the past, people who had diabetes would eat foods based on their blood sugar levels. This type of diet could cause severe health issues. In today's modern world, different types of food can be cooked in an air fryer. Since it is healthier than cooking with oil, most people have tried using an air fryer. These recipes are healthier for the body and the heart.

Diabetic people are known to live longer lives than non-diabetics. While this is not a surefire indicator of their health, it shows that blood sugar level control is of great importance. Research has shown that food cooked in an air fryer is healthier and better for controlling blood sugar levels than other cooking types.

You need to cook well to control blood sugar levels effectively as a person with diabetes. This means that you need to incorporate low on carbs and high protein into your diet. The air fryer is the ideal appliance as it cooks food safely and healthily.

Imagine eating delicious food without all the fat and calories. That's the promise of air frying. You wouldn't know you were eating.

Air frying is a healthy alternative to conventional cooking that is quickly becoming a favorite among people with diabetes and who care about their weight. It also presents an opportunity for those who do not have diabetes to enjoy healthier meals without giving up tasty foods.

That's what this cookbook has to offer. There's a lot to learn, but you won't have to do it alone. Each recipe includes information on what air fryers are, how they work, and why they are used to prepare foods instead of ordinary ovens, microwaves, or even electric stoves.

There are many benefits to a diet based on blood sugar levels. Doctors and nurses recommend that people with diabetes eat high protein foods to help regulate their blood sugar. Air fryers can produce foods that mimic this type of food to get the same benefits as if they were eating the food normally. It is easier to prepare and requires less fat to cook these foods. This is why air frying is becoming more popular among diabetics and non-diabetics alike.

Diabetic Air Fryer Cookbook is your complete guide to using air fryers safely. You learn about how they work and how they can make your life easier while still serving up tasty, healthy meals that will keep you fuller longer.

INDEX

Made in the USA
Monee, IL
14 November 2022

17705140R00052